teach® yourself

instant greek
elisabeth smith

language consultants:
dennis couniacis
howard middle

For over 60 years, more than
50 million people have learnt over
750 subjects the **teach yourself**
way, with impressive results.

be where you want to be
with **teach yourself**

The publisher has used its best endeavours to ensure that the URLs for external websites referred to in this book are correct and active at the time of going to press. However, the publisher and the author have no responsibility for the websites and can make no guarantee that a site will remain live or that the content will remain relevant, decent or appropriate.

For UK order enquiries: please contact Bookpoint Ltd, 130 Milton Park, Abingdon, Oxon OX14 4SB. Telephone: +44 (0) 1235 827720. Fax: +44 (0) 1235 400454. Lines are open 09.00–17.00, Monday to Saturday, with a 24-hour message answering service. Details about our titles and how to order are available at www.teachyourself.co.uk

For USA order enquiries: please contact McGraw-Hill Customer Services, PO Box 545, Blacklick, OH 43004-0545, USA. Telephone: 1-800-722-4726. Fax: 1-614-755-5645.

For Canada order enquiries: please contact McGraw-Hill Ryerson Ltd, 300 Water St, Whitby, Ontario L1N 9B6, Canada. Telephone: 905 430 5000. Fax: 905 430 5020.

Long renowned as the authoritative source for self-guided learning – with more than 50 million copies sold worldwide – the **teach yourself** series includes over 500 titles in the fields of languages, crafts, hobbies, business, computing and education.

British Library Cataloguing in Publication Data: a catalogue record for this title is available from the British Library.

Library of Congress Catalog Card Number: on file.

First published in UK 2000 by Hodder Education, 338 Euston Road, London, NW1 3BH.

First published in US 2000 by The McGraw-Hill Companies, Inc.

2nd edition published 2003. 3rd edition published 2006.

The **teach yourself** name is a registered trade mark of Hodder Headline.

Typeset by Transet Limited, Coventry, England.
Printed in Great Britain for Hodder Education, a division of Hodder Headline, 338 Euston Road, London, NW1 3BH, by Cox & Wyman Ltd, Reading, Berkshire.

Hodder Headline's policy is to use papers that are natural, renewable and recyclable products and made from wood grown in sustainable forests. The logging and manufacturing processes are expected to conform to the environmental regulations of the country of origin.

Impression number   10 9 8 7 6 5 4 3 2 1
Year   2010 2009 2008 2007 2006

contents

4 contents

read this first

If, like me, you usually skip introductions, don't! Read on! You need to know how **Instant Greek** works and why.

When I decided to write the **Instant** series I first called it *Barebones*, because that's what you want: *no frills, no fuss, just the bare bones and go!* So in **Instant Greek** you'll find:

• Less than 500 words to say everything, well... nearly everything.

• No ghastly grammar – just a few useful tips.

• No time wasters such as... 'the pen of my aunt...'

• No phrase book phrases for a working breakfast with the offspring of Onassis.

• No need to struggle with the Greek script – everything is in easy phonetic language.

• No need to be perfect. Mistakes won't spoil your success.

I have put some 30 years of teaching experience into this course. I know how people learn. I also know for how long they are motivated by a new project (a few weeks) and how little time they can spare to study each day (under an hour). That's why you'll complete **Instant Greek** in six weeks and get away with 45 minutes a day.

Of course there is some learning to do, but I have tried to make it as much fun as possible, even the boring bits. You'll meet Tom and Kate Walker on holiday in Greece. They do the kind of things you need to know about: shopping, eating out and getting about. As you will note, Tom and Kate speak **Instant Greek** all the time, even to each other. What paragons of virtue!

To get the most out of this course, there are only two things you really should do:

- Follow the **Day-by-day guide** as suggested. Please don't skip bits and short-change your success. Everything is there for a reason.
- If you are a complete beginner, buy the recording that accompanies this book. It will also get you to speak faster and with confidence.

When you have filled in your **Certificate** at the end of the book and can speak **Instant Greek**, I would like to hear from you. Why not visit my website www.elisabeth-smith.co.uk, e-mail me at elisabeth.smith@hodder.co.uk, or write to me care of Hodder Education, 338 Euston Road, London, NW1 3BH?

Elisabeth Smith

how this book works

Instant Greek has been structured for your rapid success. This is how it works:

Day-by-day guide Stick to it. If you miss a day, add one.

Dialogues Follow Tom and Kate through Greece. The English of Weeks 1–3 is in 'Greek-speak' to get you tuned in.

New words Don't fight them, don't skip them – learn them! The flash cards will help you.

Good news grammar After you read it you are allowed to forget half and still succeed! That's why it's good news.

Flash words and flash sentences Read about these building blocks in the flash card section on page 92. Then use them!

Learn by heart Obligatory! Memorizing puts you on the fast track to speaking in full sentences.

Let's speak Greek *You* will be doing the talking – in Greek.

Spot the keys Listen to rapid Greek and make sense of it.

Say it simply Learn how to use plain, **Instant Greek** to say what you want to say. Don't be shy!

Test your progress Mark your own test and be amazed by the result.

Answers This is where you'll find the answers to the exercises.

▶ This icon asks you to switch on the recording.

Pronunciation If you don't know about it and don't have the recording, go straight to page 15. You need to know about pronunciation before you can start Week 1.

Progress chart Enter your score each week and monitor your progress. Are you going for *very good* or *outstanding*?

Certificate It's on page 91. In six weeks it will have your name on it!

progress chart

At the end of each week record your test score on the progress chart below.

At the end of the course throw out your worst result – anybody can have a bad week – and add up your *five* best weekly scores. Divide the total by five to get your average score and overall course result.

Write your result – *outstanding, excellent, very good* or *good* – on your **Certificate**. If you scored more than 80% enlarge it and frame it!

Progress chart

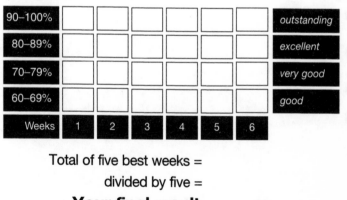

90–100%							outstanding
80–89%							excellent
70–79%							very good
60–69%							good
Weeks	1	2	3	4	5	6	

Total of five best weeks =

divided by five =

Your final result _____ %

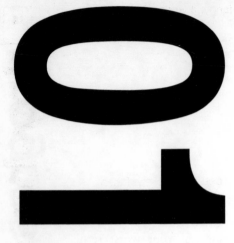

01

week one

Study for 45 minutes – or a little longer if you can!

Day zero

- Start with **Read this first**.
- Read **How this book works**.

Day one

- Read **In the aeroplane**.
- Listen to/Read **Sto aeroplano**.
- Listen to/Read the **New words**, then learn some of them.

Day two

- Repeat **Sto aeroplano** and the **New words**.
- Listen to/Read **Pronunciation**.
- Learn more **New words**.

Day three

- Learn all the **New words** until you know them well.
- Use the **Flash words** to help you.
- Read and learn the **Good news grammar**.

Day four

- Cut out and learn the **Flash sentences**.
- Listen to/Read **Learn by heart**.

Day five

- Listen to/Read **Let's speak Greek**.
- Revise! Tomorrow you'll be testing your progress.

Day six

- Listen to/Read **Let's speak more Greek** (optional).
- Listen to/Read **Let's speak Greek – fast and fluently** (optional).
- Translate **Test your progress**.

Day seven is your day off!

day-by-day guide

In the aeroplane

Tom and Kate Walker are on their way to Greece. They are
boarding flight QI 915 to Skiathos via Athens and squeeze past
Aristotelis Nikou. (*The English of Weeks 1–3 is in 'Greek-
speak' to get you tuned in.*)

Tom	Excuse me, we have the seats 9a and 9b.
Ari	Yes, sure, one moment please.
Tom	Good morning, we are the Tom and the Kate Walker.
Ari	Good morning, I am the Aristotelis.
Tom	The Aristotelis Onassis?
Ari	No, unfortunately. I am the Aristotelis Nikou.
Tom	We go to Skiathos. And you?
Ari	No, I am going to Athens. But I am from the Patras.
Tom	I was in the Patras in the April. The Patras is very beautiful. I was in the Patras for the company my.
Ari	What work do you do?
Tom	I work with computer.
Ari	And you, Mrs Walker? What do you do? Where (do) you work?
Kate	I worked at a school for three years. Now I work at the Rover.
Ari	Are you from the London?
Kate	No, we are from the Manchester. We were one year in the New York and two years in the London. Now we work in the Birmingham.
Ari	I worked for five years at the Fiat. Now I work at the Bank of Greece.
Kate	How is the work at the bank? Good?
Ari	The work is boring. I work a lot but the money is better. I need a lot of money! I have a big house, a Mercedes and four children. The wife my is American. She has a girlfriend in Florida and she is always on the telephone. It costs a lot.
Kate	Now we are on holiday. And you?
Ari	Unfortunately no. Not we are on holiday now. We are on holiday the August. Always we go to Porto Rafti but without the children. We have a house there without telephone, and we not have mobile!

▶ Sto aeroplano

Tom and Kate Walker are on their way to Greece. They are boarding flight QI 915 to Skiathos via Athens and squeeze past Aristotelis Nikou.

Tom	Signomi, exoome tis THesis enea alfa ke enea vita.
Ari	Ne, vevea, mia stigmi, parakalo.
Tom	Kalimera, imaste o Tom ke i Kate Walker.
Ari	Kalimera, ime o Aristotelis.
Tom	O Aristotelis Onassis?
Ari	Oxi, thistixos. Ime o Aristotelis Nikou.
Tom	Pame stin SkiaTHo. Ke esis?
Ari	Oxi, pao stin Athina. Ala ime apo tin Patra.
Tom	Imoona stin Patra ton Aprilio. I Patra ine poli omorfi. Imoona stin Patra ya tin eteria moo.
Ari	Ti thoolia kanete?
Tom	Thoolevo me komputer.
Ari	Ke esis, kiria Walker? Ti kanete? Poo thoolevete?
Kate	Thoolepsa se ena skolio ya tria xronia. Tora thoolevo stin Rover.
Ari	Isaste apo to Lonthino?
Kate	Oxi, imaste apo to Manchester. Imastan ena xrono stin Nea Iorki ke thio xronia sto Lonthino. Tora thoolevoome sto Birmingham.
Ari	Thoolepsa ya pende xronia stin Fiat. Tora thoolevo stin Trapeza tis Elathos.
Tom	Pos ine i thoolia stin trapeza? Kali?
Ari	I thoolia ine vareti. Thoolevo para poli ala ta lefta ine kalitera. Xriazome pola lefta! Exo ena megalo spiti, mia Mercedes ke tesera pethia. I yineka moo ine Amerikana. Exi mia fili stin Floritha ke ine sinexia sto tilefono. Kostizi poli.
Kate	Tora imaste se thiakopes. Ke esis?
Ari	Thistixos oxi. Then imaste se thiakopes tora. Imaste se thiakopes ton Avgoosto. Panda pame sto Porto Rafti ala xoris ta pethia. Exoome ena spiti eki xoris tilefono, ke then exoome kinito!

▶ New words

sto aeroplano   *in the aeroplane*
signomi   *excuse me*
exoome   *we have*
o/i/to/ta/tis/tin/ton   *the*
THesi, THesis   *seat, seats*
enea   *nine*
alfa, vita   *a, b*
ke   *and*
ne   *yes*
vevea   *sure, certain(ly)*
mia stigmi   *one moment*
parakalo   *please*
kalimera   *good morning*
imaste   *we are, we were/ have been*
ime   *I am*
oxi   *no*
thistixos   *unfortunately*
pame   *we/let's go*
sto, stin, stis   *to/at/in the*
ke esis   *and you?/you, too?*
esis   *you*
pao   *I go, I'm going*
ala   *but*
apo   *from*
imoona/imoon   *I was*
Aprilio(s)   *April*
ine   *he/she/it is*
poli   *very, much, a lot*
omorfos/i/o   *beautiful*
ya   *for*
moo   *my*
eteria   *company/firm*
ti   *what*
i thoolia   *the work*
kanete   *you do/do you do?*
thoolevo   *I work*
me   *with*
kirios, kiria   *Mr/gentleman, Mrs/lady*
poo   *where*

thoolevete   *you work/do you work?*
thoolepsa   *I worked*
se   *in, at*
enas/mia/ena   *a/one*
skolio   *school*
tria   *three*
xrono, xronia   *year, years*
tora   *now*
isaste   *you are/are you?*
thio   *two*
pende   *five*
i Trapeza tis Elathos   *the Bank of Greece*
pos   *how*
kalos/kali/kalo   *good, nice*
varetos/i/o   *boring*
poli   *a lot, para poli   too much*
lefta   *money*
kalitera   *better*
xriazome   *I need*
exo   *I have*
megalo   *big*
spiti   *house*
tesera   *four*
pethia   *children*
yineka   *woman, wife*
Amerikana   *American*
exi   *he/she/it has*
fili   *(girl)friend*
sinexia   *always*
kostizi   *it costs*
se thiakopes   *on holiday*
then   *not*
Avgoosto   *August*
panda   *always*
xoris   *without*
eki   *there*
to tilefono   *the telephone*
kinito   *mobile phone*

TOTAL NEW WORDS: 77
...only 293 words to go!

Some easy extras

Mines – months

Ianooarios, Fevrooarios, Martios, Aprilios, Maios, Ioonios, Ioolios, Avgoostos, Septemvrios, Oktovrios, Noemvrios, Thekemvrios

Arithmi – numbers

0 = mithen		6 = eksi	
1 = ena		7 = epta	
2 = thio		8 = okto	
3 = tria		9 = enea	
4 = tesera		10 = theka	
5 = pende			

More greetings

kalispera *good evening*; ya/yasoo (sing)/yasas (pl) *hello, goodbye/'bye*; kalinixta *good night*; adio *goodbye*

▶ Pronunciation

The Greek language is beautiful, so drop all inhibitions and try to speak **Greek** rather than English with the words changed. If Greek pronunciation is new to you **please buy the recording** and listen to the real thing.

As you can see, all the words in **Instant Greek** have been transliterated into phonetic language. That makes it much easier to learn, especially if you are in a hurry. You don't have to learn the Greek script first but can start speaking straight away.

As Greek is a Mediterranean language the vowels in Greek are similar to Italian or Spanish and are explained below.

The vowels

The English word in brackets gives you an example of the sound. Say the sound OUT LOUD and then the Greek examples OUT LOUD.

a (hat) Amerikana	e (yes) exi	i (feet) spiti
o (not) pos	oo (pool) thoolia	

The consonants

Most consonants are pronounced as in English.

'TH' and 'th' represent two distinct sounds in Greek:

   TH as in English *thin* (THesis *seats*)
   th as in English *there* (then exoome *we don't have*)

'x' represents the Greek sound 'kh', similar to, but stronger than, the English 'h'.

You don't have to think too hard about it all – just go ahead!

Stress

In this book, the letter in **bold** type tells you to stress the syllable in which it appears, for example, ehume, parakalo, kiria. Always say the words **OUT LOUD**. That way you'll remember where the accent goes.

When you go to Greece you'll want to know a little of the script, too. So, as an introduction, here's the Greek alphabet. And later in the course there'll also be a few useful flash words in 'real' Greek script, to help you on your way!

   Α Β Γ Δ Ε Ζ Η Θ Ι Κ Λ Μ Ν Ξ Ο Π Ρ Σ Τ Υ Φ Χ Ψ Ω
   α β γ δ ε ζ η θ ι κ λ μ ν ξ ο π ρ σ τ υ φ χ ψ ω

▶ Good news grammar

This is the good news part of each week. Remember, I promised: no ghastly grammar! I simply explain the differences between Greek and English. This will help you to speak Greek **instantly!**

1 Names of things (nouns)

There are three kinds of noun in Greek: *masculine, feminine* and *neuter*.

You can tell which is which by the word **o, i** or **to** in front of the word.

You can also tell by the ending of the noun:

Most masculine words end in -os or -as: o yatros (*the doctor*), o anthras (*the man*).

Most feminine words end in -a or -i: i thoolia, mia stigmi.

Most neuter words end in -o or -i: to tilefono, to spiti.

The adjective describing the noun also ends in -os (*masculine*), -i (*feminine*) or -o (*neuter*). So *the good man, the good work* or *the good house* would be: o kalos anthras, i kali thoolia, to kalo spiti.

When you talk about more than one thing (plural) **o, i, to** change into **i, i, ta** and the endings of the nouns also change, to **-i, -es** or **-a**.

Example: i kali anthres, i kales thoolies and ta kala spitia.

This is beginning to sound very complicated, and I don't expect you to learn it or remember it all. You'll pick it up as you go along, without even noticing it! And the best news is, if you muddle things up and make a mistake and say: to kala spitia or o kali anthres, people will not throw a fit but still understand you perfectly well!

2 Doing things (verbs)

Unlike the English, Greeks do not use the *I, you, he, she, it, we* or *they* persons, to identify who is doing something unless they wish to clarify or stress it. So the only way you can tell **who** it is that is doing something is from the **verb itself**. Each person has his, her or its own verb form and ending. Occasionally a verb ending is shared which could lead to some confusion, but amazingly enough it works out all right once it's in a sentence.

There are a few verbs which you'll use every day. I have put the first two of these into a 'gift box' below. Learn them now until you can say them with your eyes closed. It won't take long!

to be	
ime	*I am*
isaste	*you are*
ine	*he/she/it is*
imaste	*we are*
ine	*they are*

to have	
exo	*I have*
exete	*you have*
exi	*he/she/it has*
exoome	*we have*
exoone	*they have*

3 the Tom, the Kate, the company my

Did you notice? An extra *the* keeps on popping up everywhere in front of nouns and names: Imaste o Tom ke i Kate Walker (*We are the Tom and the Kate Walker*).

When you want to say: *for my company*, you can't just say literally: ya moo eteria. As you will see in the following section, you have to shuffle things around – adding *the* in front of the noun and putting *my* after the noun – and say:

ya tin eteria moo: *for the company my*

Sounds rather grand doesn't it?... o Charles; o komputer moo.

Moo, sas, too, tis

When Greeks say *my, your, his, her*, they always add o, i or to depending on whether the word which follows is masculine (male), feminine (female) or neuter (neither male nor female).

So as well as: o komputer moo, they say i efimeritha moo (*my newspaper*), and to aftokinito too (*his car*).

4 Two into one

Greeks love their language to be as smooth as possible. Little pairs of words like *to the* sound too 'staccato' to them so they 'melt' the two words into one. Here are three examples:

se+to = sto   se+ton = ston   se+tin = stin

And if you don't 'melt'? No problem. People will still understand you.

There are three forms of the Greek for 'in (the)', depending on the gender of the city name in Greek:

ston Volo (Volos is masculine)
stin Nea Yorki (New York is feminine)
sto Parisi (Paris is neuter)

▶ Learn by heart

Don't be tempted to skip this exercise because it reminds you of school... If you want to speak, not stumble, saying a few lines by HEART does the trick!

Learn **Kalimera** by HEART after you have filled in the gaps with your personal, or any, information. Say **Kalimera** aloud and fairly fast. Can you beat 40 seconds?

Kalimera

Kalimera, ime o/i ....*(name)*
Ime apo to(n)/ti(n) ....*(place)*
Imoona sto ....*(place)* ton ....*(month)*
Thoolepsa ya tin ....*(firm)* ya thio xronia.
Tora thoolevo stin..*(place)*
Exo ena megalo spiti stin/sto ....*(place)*. Kostizi poli.
Ton Avgoosto pame stin/sto ....*(place)*.
Pos ine i ATHina ton Aprilio? Omorfi? ....

▶ Let's speak Greek

Here are ten English sentences. Read each sentence and say it in Greek – OUT LOUD! Check your answer below before you try the next sentence. If you have the recording, listen to **Let's speak Greek** to check your answers.

1 Are you from London?
2 Yes, I am from London.
3 I am on holiday in August.
4 We are going to Corfu (Kerkira).
5 I was in Athens for my firm.
6 Do you have a Ferrari?
7 No – unfortunately!
8 We have a house in Athens.
9 How is the job with Fiat, good?
10 No, it is boring, but the money is better.

Well, how many did you get right? If you are not happy do it again! Here are some questions in Greek. Answer them in Greek. Start every answer with **Ne**, and talk about yourself.

11 **I**saste ap**o** to Manchester?
12 **E**xete spiti sto Lonthino?
13 **P**ame stin K**e**rkira. Ke esis?
14 Thool**e**vete stin Trapeza tis El**a**thos?
15 **E**xete kali thool**i**a?

Now tell someone in Greek…

16 …that you have two children.
17 …that you were in Athens.
18 …that you have a Fiat Uno.
19 …that you are going to Skiathos.
20 …that Birmingham is boring in November.

Answers

1 **I**saste ap**o** to Lonthino?
2 Ne, ime ap**o** to Lonthino.
3 Ime se thiakopes ton **A**vgoosto.
4 Pame stin Kerkira.
5 Imoona stin ATHina ya tin eteria moo.
6 **E**xete mia Ferrari?
7 **O**xi – thistixos!
8 Exoome ena spiti stin ATHina.
9 Pos ine i thoolia me tin Fiat, kali?
10 **O**xi, ine vareti, ala ta lefta ine kalitera.

11 Ne, ime ap**o** to Manchester.
12 Ne, **e**xo spiti sto Lonthino.
13 Ne, ke ego pao stin Kerkira.
14 Ne, thoolevo ya tin Trapeza tis Elathos.
15 Ne, **e**xo kali thoolia.
16 **E**xo thio pethia.
17 Imoona stin ATHina.
18 **E**xo ena Fiat Uno.
19 Pao stin Skiatho.
20 To Birmingham ine varet**o** ton Noemvrio.

Well, what was your score? If you got 20 ticks you can give yourself a triple star!

▶ Let's speak more Greek

Here are some optional exercises. They may stretch the 45 minutes a day by 15 minutes. But the extra practice will be worth it.

And always remember: near enough is good enough!

In your own words

This exercise will teach you to express yourself freely. Use only the words you have learned so far.

Tell me in your own words that...

Example you are Peter Smith
         Ime o Peter Smith.

1 you are from Manchester
2 you have an American (female) friend
3 you are a workaholic...
4 ...but you don't have a lot of cash
5 you have two children
6 the children are six and eight
7 unfortunately you work with PCs; the work is not interesting
8 your wife spends a lot of time on the phone
9 you own a property in Athens
10 you are on holiday without the children

Answers

1 Ime apo to Manchester.
2 Exo mia fili Amerikana.
3 Thoolevo sinexia.../Thoolevo para poli...
4 ...ala then exo pola lefta.
5 Exo/exoome thio pethia.
6 Ta pethia ine eksi ke okto.
7 Thistixos thoolevo me komputer. I thoolia ine vareti.
8 I yineka moo ine sinexia sto tilefono.
9 Exo/exume ena spiti stin ATHina.
10 Ime/Imaste se thiakopes xoris ta pethia.

▶ Let's speak Greek – fast and fluently

No more stuttering and stumbling! Get out the stopwatch and time yourself with this fluency practice.

Translate each section and check if it is correct, then cover up the answers and say the three or four sentences fast!

20 seconds per section for a silver star, 15 seconds for a gold star.

Some of the English is in 'Greek-speak' to help you.

Good evening. I am going to Athens. You, too?
No, I work in Patras – for a bank. But I am going to Skiathos.
I am on holiday – without computer.

Kalispera. Pao stin ATHina. Ke esis?
Oxi, thoolevo stin Patra – ya mia trapeza. Ala pao stin SkiaTHo.
Ime se thiakopes – xoris komputer.

How is Skiathos? Is it big?
No, it is not big, but it is not boring.
It is very beautiful in June.
A house in Skiathos costs a lot of money.

Pos ine i SkiaTHos? Ine megali?
Oxi, then ine megali, ala then ine vareti.
Ine poli omorfi ton Ioonio.
Ena spiti stin SkiaTHo kostizi pola lefta.

I have a girlfriend, (the) Nana.
She has a house in Athens.
Oh, excuse me. One moment, please, it is (the) Nana.
She is always on the phone. 'Bye!

Exo mia fili, tin Nana.
Exi ena spiti stin ATHina.
O, signomi. Mia stigmi, parakalo, ine i Nana.
Ine panda sto tilefono. Yiasas!

Now say **all** the sentences in Greek without stopping and starting.

If you can do it in under one minute you are a fast and fluent winner!

But if you are not happy with your result – just try once more.

Test your progress

This is your only written exercise. You'll be amazed at how easy it is! Translate the 20 sentences without looking at the previous pages.

Don't try to show the stress/accent when you write. That would take you forever!

1 Good morning, we are Ari and Jane.
2 I am from Athens, and you?
3 Where (do) you work now?
4 I was in Athens in October.
5 My girlfriend is in Greece for one year.
6 We always go to Rhodes (**R**otho) in June.
7 I worked at Fiat in May.
8 What (do) you do in London?
9 I work in a school.
10 The big house in Porto Rafti is for the children.
11 One moment please, where is Aristotelis?
12 (Does) the house have a telephone? No, unfortunately (not).
13 (Does) a Ferrari cost a lot? Yes, sure, it costs too much.
14 How is the work in Greece, good?
15 Aristotelis has a girlfriend in my firm.
16 We have been in Skiathos for three days.
17 We have good seats in (the) aeroplane.
18 I always have boring holidays.
19 He has a beautiful wife, a Lamborghini and a lot of money.
20 Are you (the) Mrs Onassis? You have a big aeroplane.

When you have finished, look up the answers on page 86 and mark your work. Then enter your result on the **Progress Chart** on page 9. If your score is higher than 80% you'll have done very well indeed!

02

week two

45 minutes a day – but a little extra will step up your progress!

25

Day one

- Read **In Koukounaries**.
- Listen to/Read **Stis Koukounaries**.
- Listen to/Read the **New words**. Learn 20 easy ones.

Day two

- Repeat **Stis Koukounaries** and the **New words**.
- Learn the harder **New words**.
- Use the **Flash words** to help you.

Day three

- Learn all the **New words** until you know them well.
- Read and learn the **Good news grammar**.

Day four

- Cut out and learn the **Flash sentences**.
- Listen to/Read **Learn by heart**.

Day five

- Listen to/Read **Let's speak Greek**.
- Go over **Learn by heart**.

Day six

- Listen to/Read **Let's speak more Greek** (optional).
- Listen to/Read **Let's speak Greek – fast and fluently** (optional).
- Translate **Test your progress**.

Day seven is a study-free day!

day-by-day guide

In Koukounaries

In Skiathos Tom and Kate hire a car and drive to Koukounaries. They speak to Anna Pavlithi of 'Hotel Pavlithi' and later, to Andreas, the waiter. (*The English of Weeks 1–3 is in 'Greek-speak' to get you tuned in.*)

Kate	Good morning. (Do) you have a double room for one night, and no(t) too expensive?
Anna	Yes, we have a double room, a little small, with bath and shower. The shower doesn't work, maybe the husband my is able to it fix.
Tom	Where is the room?
Anna	It is here, left. Is it enough big?
Tom	It is a little small, but not bad. How much (does) it cost?
Anna	Only 100 euros for two, but no credit cards! The breakfast is from the eight until nine and half.
Tom	OK. We'll take it. But are we able to have breakfast at eight less quarter? Tomorrow at eight and quarter we want to go to the Axlathies.
Kate	Excuse me, where can we to drink something? Is there a bar here near?
Anna	There are two bars five minutes from here. It is not difficult. Thirty metres right and then straight on.

(in the bar)

Andreas	What do you want?
Kate	We want a coffee and a tea with milk.
Andreas	(Do) you want something to eat?
Tom	What (do) you have?
Andreas	We have apple pie or bread rolls.
Kate	Two bread rolls with ham, please.
Tom	The ham not is good.
Kate	The ham my is very good.
Tom	The table is very small.
Kate	But the toilet is big and very clean.
Tom	The tea is cold.
Kate	But the waiter is handsome.
Tom	Waiter! The bill, please!
Andreas	15 euros, please.

▶ Stis Koukounaries

In Skiathos Tom and Kate hire a car and drive to Koukounaries.
They speak to Anna Pavlithi of 'Hotel Pavlithi' and later, to
Andreas, the waiter.

Kate	Kalimera. Exete ena thiklino ya mia nixta, ke oxi poli akrivo?
Anna	Ne, exoome ena thiklino, ligo mikro, me banio ke doosh. To doosh then thoolevi, isos o anthras moo bori na to ftiaksi.
Tom	Poo ine to thomatio?
Anna	Ine etho, aristera. Ine arketa megalo?
Tom	Ine ligo mikro, ala oxi asximo. Poso kostizi?
Anna	Mono ekato evro ya thio, ala oxi pistotikes kartes! To proino ine apo tis okto mexri tis enea ke misi.
Tom	Endaksi. To pernoome. Ala boroome na exoome proino stis okto para tetarto? Avrio stis okto ke tetarto theloome na pame stis Axlathies.
Kate	Signomi, poo boroome na pioome kati? Exi kanena bar etho konda?
Anna	Ine thio bar pende lepta apo etho. Then ine thiskolo. Trianda metra theksia ke meta isia.
(sto bar)	
Andreas	Ti THelete?
Kate	THeloome enan kafe ke ena tsai me gala.
Andreas	THelete kati na fate?
Tom	Ti exete?
Andreas	Exoome milopita i psomakia.
Kate	Thio psomakia me zambon, parakalo.
Tom	To zambon then ine kalo.
Kate	To zambon moo ine poli kalo.
Tom	To trapezi ine poli mikro.
Kate	Ala i tooaleta ine megali ke poli kaTHari.
Tom	To tsai ine krio.
Kate	Ala o servitoros ine omorfos.
Tom	Servitore! Ton logariasmo, parakalo!
Andreas	Thekapende evro, parakalo.

▶ New words

Learning words the traditional way can be boring. If you enjoyed the flash cards why not make your own for the rest of the words. Always say the word OUT LOUD. It's the fast track to speaking!

thom**a**tio   *room*
thi**kli**no   *double room*
i **ni**xta   *the night*
akriv**o**   *expensive*
l**i**go   *little*
mikr**os/i/o**   *small*
b**a**nio   *bath*
d**oo**sh   *shower*
isos   *perhaps*
anthras   *husband/man*
bor**i** (na fti**a**ksi…)   *he/she/it can (fix…)*
eth**o**   *here*
arister**a**   *left*
ark**e**ta   *enough*
oxi **a** schimo/a   *not bad*
p**o**so kost**i**zi   *how much does it cost?*
m**o**no   *only*
ekat**o**   *(a) hundred*
evr**o**   *euro, euros*
pistotik**e**s k**a**rtes   *credit cards*
proin**o**   *breakfast*
m**e**chri   *until*
mis**o**/mis**i**   *half*
end**a**ksi   *OK*
pern**oo**me   *we take*
bor**oo**me (na)   *we can*
(na) **e**xoome proin**o**   *(to) have breakfast (we)*
par**a**   *less/before (with time)*
ke   *and/past (with time)*
t**e**tarto   *quarter*

avrio   *tomorrow*
TH**e**loome (na)   *we want/we'd like*
pi**oo**me   *drink (we)*
k**a**ti   *something*
kan**e**na   *none/any (things)*
k**o**nda   *near*
lept**o**/lept**a**   *minute, minutes*
thi**sko**los/i/o   *difficult*
tri**a**nda   *30*
m**e**tra   *metres*
theksi**a**   *right*
m**e**ta   *then*
isia   *straight on*
sto bar   *in the bar*
ti TH**e**lete?   *what would you like? (lit. what (do) you want?)*
kaf**e**s/kaf**e**   *coffee*
ts**a**i   *tea*
g**a**la   *milk*
k**a**ti na f**a**te   *something to eat*
mil**o**pita   *apple pie*
i   *or*
psom**a**ki, psom**a**kia   *bread roll/rolls (little/small bread)*
zamb**o**n   *ham*
trap**e**zi   *table*
i too**a**leta, too**a**letes   *the toilet(s)*
kaTHar**os/i/o**   *clean*
kr**i**os/a/o   *cold*
servit**o**ros   *waiter*
logariasm**o**s   *bill*
thekap**e**nde   *15*

TOTAL NEW WORDS: 60
…only 233 words to go!

Some useful extras

Arithmi – more numbers

11 en**theka**	19 thekae**nea**	60 ek**sinda**
12 tho**theka**	20 i**kosi**	70 evtho**minda**
13 theka**tria**	21 ikosi**ena**	80 og**thonda**
14 theka**tesera**	22 ikosi**thio**	90 ene**ninda**
15 theka**pende**	23 ikosi**tria**	100 e**kato**
16 theka**eksi**	30 tri**anda**	200 thia**kosia**
17 theka**epta**	40 sa**randa**	1000 **xilia**
18 theka**okto**	50 pe**ninda**	

I ora – the time

ti **ora**?	*at what time?*	
stis **pende**?	*at five o'clock?*	
ine **mia**	*it's one o'clock*	
ine **thio**	*it's two o'clock*	
ena **lepto**	*a minute*	
	(just a minute)	

mia **ora**   *an hour*
mia **mera**   *a day*
mia evtho**matha**   *a week*
enas **minas**   *a month*
enas **xronos**   *a year*
too xro**noo**   *next year*

half past = ke **misi**

quarter past = ke te**tarto**

quarter to = para te**tarto**

► Good news grammar

1 I, you, he/she/it, we, they

In Greek these are: ego, esis, aftos/afti/afto, emis and afti. As you know, they are only used for emphasis: *I do this, you did that.*

Although there is no particular way to know immediately whether afti on its own means *she* or *they*, when it is used in a sentence, it becomes obvious.

Esis is the formal and polite way of saying *you*. You use it when you are talking to someone you don't know, someone in authority, and more than one person. When in Greece and speaking **Instant Greek** always use esis. There is also esi for family and friends but that needs a lot more grammar. Leave that till next year.

2 Saying *then* (not)

Did you notice in Week 1 what happened to the *not* when o Ari Nikou said: 'Then imaste se thiakopes tora?' (**not** we are on holiday now). The *not* moved in front of the verb. It does this all the time:

I thoolia ine kali. I thoolia then ine kali. (*The work is good. The work not is good*).

3 Verbs (again)

This week's good news: two more everyday verbs – **go** and **can** – in 'gift boxes', for easy learning. You'll need only a few minutes this time, because there is a bit of a pattern to each verb:

I usually ends in -o: exo, kano, thoolevo
You ends in -ete (or -ite): exete, kanete, thoolevete, borite
He/she/it ends in -i: exi, kani, thoolevi
We ends in -oome: exoome, kanoome, thoolevoome
They ends in -oon or -oone: exoon(e), kanoon(e), thoolevoon(e)

Simple, isn't it?

Here's an example: **kano** (*I do*) in a gift box!

I	*you*	*he/she/it*	*we*	*they*
kano	**kanete**	**kani**	**kanoome**	**kanoon(e)**

There are a total of 30 verbs in **Instant Greek** and 21 of these are 'regular', which means they follow the above pattern.

That leaves you with nine 'rebels' – verbs which make their own rules. You have learnt two rebels already – **exo** and **ime**, *have* and *be*. Here's one more: **pao** (*go*). Then there's **boro** (*can*) – a useful fellow and member of the good verbs team.

Spend five minutes on each.

pao	*I go*
pate	*you go*
pai	*he/she/it goes*
pame	*we go*
pane	*they go*

bor**o** (na)	*I can*
bor**ite** (na)	*you can*
bor**i** (na)	*he/she/it can*
bor**oo**me (na)	we can
bor**oo**ne (na)	*they can*

4 A recap

While you are in the swing of things let's recap on the rest of the regular verbs which you have learnt so far. Once you know how to say **I** … *work/fix/take/drink/want (would like)*, you know the pattern, and you can say the rest.

So now take these five on board, too:

thoolevo – ftiaxno – perno – pino – THelo

5 A bonus

In Greek the same verbs are used for whether it's an action you **do** or an action you **are doing**. Therefore *I go* and *I am going* would be: pao and pao. That makes things a lot simpler!

▶ Let's speak Greek

Now let's practise what you have learnt. Here are ten English sentences for you to say in Greek OUT LOUD! After each sentence check to see if you got it right. If you didn't, do the exercise again.

1 We would like a room.
2 At what time is there breakfast?
3 The telephone does not work.
4 How much is (costs) the room?
5 Where is the bar, on the right or on the left?
6 Is there (do you have) something to eat?
7 All right, we take it.
8 Can we go to Athens?
9 We would like to go at half past two.
10 Excuse me, the bill please.

Now answer in Greek. Use **ne** and speak about yourself.

11 Thoolevete stis okto ke misi?
12 THelete ena psomaki?
13 Exete pola lefta?

Now answer with **oxi** and speak for yourself and a friend.

14 Exete ena trapezi ya pende?
15 Exete peninda evro?
16 Exete tsai me gala?

And now answer freely. Your answers may differ from mine but still be correct.

17 Poo ine to ksenothoxio (hotel) Aliki?
18 Poo ine to thomatio?
19 Poo ine to bar?
20 Poso kostizi to tilefono?

Answers

1 THeloome ena thomatio.
2 Ti ora ine to proino?
3 To tilefono then thoolevi.
4 Poso kostizi to thomatio?
5 Poo ine to bar, theksia i aristera?
6 Exete kati na fame?
7 Endaksi, to pernoome.
8 Boroome na pame stin ATHina?
9 THeloome na pame stis thio ke misi.
10 Signomi, ton logariasmo, parakalo.

11 Ne, thoolevo stis okto ke misi.
12 Ne, THelo ena psomaki.
13 Ne, exo pola lefta.
14 Oxi, then exoome ena trapezi ya pende.
15 Oxi, then exoome peninda evro.
16 Oxi, then exoome tsai me gala.
17 To ksenothoxio Aliki ine stin Patra.
18 Ine theksia ke meta isia.
19 Ine isia ke meta aristera.
20 Kostizi para poli.

▶ Let's speak more Greek

Here are the two optional exercises. Remember, they may stretch the 45 minutes a day by 15 minutes. But the extra practice will be worth it.

In your own words

This exercise will teach you to express yourself freely.

Use only the words you have learned so far.

Ask me in your own words...

1 if there is availability of a double room en suite
2 what the price of the room is for one night
3 where you can have a coffee

Tell me...

4 that there is a bar at 20 minutes from here, straight ahead
5 you would like breakfast at 7.30
6 you are thinking of going to Corfu tomorrow
7 you want one coffee and apple pie
8 what you don't like about the café (the table is too small and the ham isn't good)
9 what Kate likes about the café (the toilets are clean and the waiter is very handsome)
10 that the bill is € 9.60

Answers

1 Signomi. Exete ena thiklino me banio?
2 Poso kostizi to thomatio ya mia nixta?
3 Poo boroome na pioome enan kafe?
4 Exi ena bar ikosi lepta apo etho, isia.
5 THeloome to proino stis efta ke misi.
6 THeloome na pame stin Kerkira avrio.
7 THeloome enan kafe ke mia milopita.
8 Then ine kala etho. To trapezi ine poli mikro ke to zambon then ine kalo.
9 I Kate lei: Ine kala etho. I tooaletes ine kaTHeres ke o servitoros ine omorfos.
10 O logariasmos ine enea evro ke eksinda lepta.

▶ Let's speak Greek – fast and fluently

No more stuttering and stumbling! Get out the stopwatch and time yourself with this fluency practice.

Translate each section and check if it is correct, then cover up the answers and say the three or four sentences fast!

20 seconds per section for a silver star, 15 seconds for a gold star.

Some of the English is in 'Greek-speak' to help you.

Good evening, do you have a room with bath?
80 euros is a little expensive.
We take a double room with shower.
How much is the breakfast? Can we have breakfast at 7 o'clock?

Kalispera. Exete ena thomatio me banio?
Ogthonda evro ine ligo akrivo.
Pernoome ena thiklino me doosh.
Poso kostizi to proino? Boroome na exoome proino stis epta?

Where is my house? Straight on, then 50 metres right.
But we are going tomorrow to Patras.
We would like to go at half past nine.

Poo ine to spiti moo? Isia, meta peninda metra theksia.
Ala avrio pame stin Patra.
THeloome na pame stis enea ke misi.

The bar here is very small and very expensive.
But the coffee is good, and the rolls with ham are not bad.
The bill, please. How much? 30 euros for one coffee and two rolls?
We do not have enough money!

To bar etho ine poli mikro ke poli akrivo.
Ala o kafes ine kalos, ke ta psomakia me zambon then ine asxima.
Ton logariasmo, parakalo. Poso? Trianda evro ya enan kafe ke thio psomakia?
Then exoome arketa lefta.

Now say **all** the sentences in Greek without stopping and starting.

If you can do it in under a minute you are a fast and fluent winner!

But if you are not happy with your result – just try once more.

▶ Learn by heart

Learn the eight lines **Then exo pola lefta…** by HEART. Try to say them with a bit of 'drama' in 40 seconds! Choose one of these to fill the gap: o anthras moo, i yineka moo, o filos (*male friend*) moo, i fili moo. But here you need to change these words to: ton anthra moo, tin yineka moo, ton filo moo, tin fili moo.

Then exo pola lefta…
Then exo pola lefta ala THelo*/THeloome na pao/pame thiakopes me…
THeloome na pame stin ATHina me to Rover.
Ine poli omorfi ton Aprilio.
To ksenothoxio** Pavlithi then ine poli akrivo.
Poso kostizi?
Mono ekato evro tin nixta.
Boroome na pame? Oxi.
Panda exi poli thoolia ke to Rover then thoolevi.

---

*thelo: *I would like*   **ksenothoxio: *hotel*

Test your progress

Translate in writing. What do you remember without looking back?

1 Where is (there) a telephone?
2 Excuse me, we only have credit cards.
3 Can we go at seven tomorrow?
4 Do you have (a) enough big table? We are five.
5 The small rooms do not have (a) bath.
6 We would like to eat ham and rolls.
7 We can go from (the) six to (the) quarter to seven.
8 Where can we drink something here near?
9 We were in the bar from nine to half past ten.
10 All right, we take the Rover for a day.
11 How much does the breakfast cost? Only 10 euros.
12 What (do) you want? The computer? It is not working.
13 How is the apple pie? Good but expensive?
14 Where are the toilets, on the left or on the right?
15 I can go to Hollywood.
16 A coffee, please… we drink too much coffee!
17 Where is (the) Mrs Pavlithi? Perhaps in the bar?
18 Six euros for a cold tea? It is a little expensive!
19 I was in Rhodes in February. It is not bad.
20 There are 300 bars here, one is (at) 30 metres on the right.

The answers are on page 87. The **Progress chart** awaits your score!

03

week three

Study for 45 minutes a day – but there are no penalties for doing more!

Day one

- Read **Let's go shopping**.
- Listen to/Read **Pame ya psonia**.
- Listen to/Read the **New words**, then learn some of them.

Day two

- Repeat **Pame ya psonia** and the **New words**.
- Learn all the **New words**. Use the **Flash cards**!

Day three

- Test yourself on all the **New words** – boring, boring, but you are over half-way already!
- Listen to/Read **Spot the keys**.
- Learn the **Good news grammar**.

Day four

- Go over the **Good news grammar**.
- Cut out and learn the ten **Flash sentences**.

Day five

- Listen to/Read **Let's speak Greek**.
- Listen to/Read **Learn by heart**.

Day six

- Listen to/Read **Let's speak more Greek** (optional).
- Listen to/Read **Let's speak Greek – fast and fluently** (optional).
- Go over **Learn by heart**.
- Have a quick look at the **New words**, weeks 1–3.
- You now know over 200 words! Well, more or less.
- Translate **Test your progress**.

Day seven – enjoy your day off!

day-by-day guide

Let's go shopping

Tom and Kate are in Porto Rafti near Athens. They have rented a summer apartment for a week. Kate plans to do some shopping, but Tom has other ideas... (*The English of Weeks 1–3 is in 'Greek-speak' to get you tuned in.*)

Kate   Today we must do the shopping. Let's go into the centre with the bus.

Tom   But there is bad weather, it makes cold and there is a lot of sport on television – the golf at two and a half.

Kate   I am sorry, but we must go first to the cash dispenser and to the post office or kiosk for stamps... then to the chemist's and to the dry cleaner's.

Tom   In that case, no golf... perhaps the football at four and a quarter. This is all?

Kate   No, we have to go to a department store to buy a new suitcase. Then I have to go to the supermarket and to the hairdresser's. And afterwards I want to buy shoes.

Tom   Good grief! Until when are the shops open?

Kate   Until the seven and half, I believe.

Tom   Then no football... perhaps the tennis at the eight.

(*Later*)

Kate   Hello Tom, here is the shopping: 200g ham, a piece cheese, half a kilo apples, two kilos potatoes, feta cheese, sugar, bread, butter, some eggs, six beers and a bottle (of) wine. I have bought too many things.

Tom   It doesn't matter. Yesterday we not ate much. And what is in the big bag? Something for me?

Kate   Well, near to the Notos Galleries there was a small shop and I saw some shoes which were the number (size) my. Not are they beautiful? White and blue. The sales assistant was very nice and handsome like the Tom Cruise.

Tom   Who is the Tom Cruise? And how much cost the shoes?

Kate   They were a little expensive, but they cost the same in the England – 360 euros.

Tom   What? The wife my is crazy!

Kate   But this the T-shirt for the golf was very cheap. Size 42, only 27 euros. Here is a newspaper in the English and now not has tennis in the TV?

▶ Pame ya psonia

Tom and Kate are in Porto Rafti near Athens. They have rented a summer apartment for a week. Kate plans to do some shopping, but Tom has other ideas…

Kate Simera prepi na kanoome ta psonia. Pame sto kendro me to leoforio.

Tom Ala o keros ine kakos, kani krio ke exi poli spor stin tileorasi – to golf stis thio ke misi.

Kate Lipame, ala prepi na pame prota stin mixani analipsis ke sto taxithromio i sto periptero ya gramatosima… meta sto farmakio ke sto stegnokaTHaristirio.

Tom Etsi, oxi golf… isos to pothosfero stis teseris ke tetarto. Afto ine olo?

Kate Oxi, prepi na pame se ena polikatastima na agorasoome mia kenooryia valitsa. Meta prepi na pao sto soopermarket ke sto komotirio. Ke meta THelo na agoraso papootsia.

Tom THee moo! Mexri pote ine ta magazia anixta?

Kate Mexri tis epta ke misi, pistevo.

Tom Etsi oxi pothosfero… isos to tenis stis okto.
(*Argotera*)

Kate Yasoo Tom, etho ine ta psonia: thiakosia gramaria zambon, ena komati tiri, miso kilo mila, thio kila patates, feta, zaxari, psomi, vootiro, merika avga, eksi bires ke ena bookali krasi. Agorasa para pola pragmata.

Tom Then pirazi. XTHes then fagame poli. Ke ti ine stin megali tsanda? Kati ya mena?

Kate Lipon, konda sto Notos Galleries itan ena mikro magazi ke itha kati papootsia poo itan sto noomero moo. Then ine omorfa? Aspra ke ble. O politis itan poli kalos ke omorfos san ton Tom Cruise.

Tom Pios ine o Tom Cruise? Ke poso kostisan ta papootsia?

Kate Itan ligo pio akriva, ala kostizoon to ithio stin Anglia – triakosia eksinda evro.

Tom Ti? I yineka moo ine treli!

Kate Ala afto to bloozaki ya to golf itan poli ftino. Noomero sarandathio, mono ikosi epta evro. Etho ine mia efimeritha sta Anglika, ke tora then exi tenis stin tileorasi?

▶ New words

Learn the **New words** in half the time using flash cards. There are 24 to start you off. Get a friend to make the rest!

ta ps**o**nia   *the shopping*
s**i**mera   *today*
pr**e**pi na   *we must*
kan**oo**me   *do (we)*
k**e**ndro   *centre*
leof**o**rio   *bus*
k**e**ros   *weather; time*
kak**os/ia/o**   *bad*
k**a**ni kri**o**   *it is cold*
   (lit. it makes cold)
i tile**o**rasi   *the television*
lip**a**me   *I'm sorry*
pr**o**ta   *first*
mixan**i** an**a**lipsis   *cash machine*
taxithr**o**mio   *post office*
per**i**ptero   *kiosk (it sells stamps)*
met**a**   *then, afterwards*
gramat**o**sima   *stamps*
farmak**i**o   *chemist's*
stegnokaTHarist**i**rio   *dry cleaner's*
etsi   *therefore, in that case*
poth**o**sfero   *football*
aft**os/i/o**   *this*
olos, **o**li, **o**lo, **o**li, **o**les, **o**la   *all*
polikat**a**stima   *department store*
agoras**oo**me   *buy (we)*
ken**oo**ryios/a/o   *new*
val**i**tsa   *suitcase*
to komot**i**rio   *the hairdresser's*
TH**e**lo   *I want*
mag**a**zi, mag**a**zia   *shop, shops*
agor**a**so   *buy (I)*
ta pap**oo**tsia   *the shoes*
TH**ee** moo!   *good grief!*
p**o**te   *when?*
an**i**xta   *open*
pist**e**vo   *I believe/think*
arg**o**tera   *later*

gram**a**ria   *grams*
kom**a**ti   *piece*
tir**i**   *cheese*
kil**o**   *kilo*
pat**a**tes   *potatoes*
z**a**xari   *sugar*
psom**i**   *bread*
v**oo**tiro   *butter*
merik**i/es/a**   *some, several*
avg**o**, avg**a**   *egg, eggs*
b**i**ra, b**i**res   *beer, beers*
book**a**li   *bottle*
kras**i**   *wine*
agor**a**sa   *I bought, I have bought*
p**a**ra pol**a**   *too many*
pr**a**gma, pr**a**gmata   *thing, things*
then p**i**razi   *it doesn't matter*
xTH**e**s   *yesterday*
fag**a**me   *we ate, have eaten*
ts**a**nda   *bag*
m**e**na   *me*
lip**o**n   *well...*
to N**o**tos Galleries   *a well-known Greek department store*
itan   *was/were*
itha   *I saw*
n**oo**mero   *size, number*
aspros/i/o   *white*
bl**e**   *blue*
pol**i**tis   *sales assistant*
san   *like*
pi**o**s?, pi**a**?, pi**o**?   *who?, which?*
kostiz**oo**n   *they cost*
to **i**thio   *the same*
Angl**i**a   *England*
trel**os/i/o**   *crazy*

bloozaki	*T-shirt*	mia efimeritha	*a newspaper*
ftino	*cheap*	sta Anglika	*in English*

TOTAL NEW WORDS: 76
...only 157 words to go!

More extras

Ta xromata – colours

aspro	*white*	kitrino	*yellow*
mavro	*black*	kafe	*brown*
kokino	*red*	gri	*grey*
ble	*blue*	portokali	*orange*
prasino	*green*	roz	*pink*

▶ Spot the keys

By now you can say many things in Greek. But what happens if you ask a question and don't understand the answer – hitting you at the speed of an automatic rifle? The smart way is not to panic, but to listen only for the words you know. Any familiar words which you pick up will provide you with key words – clues to what the other person is saying. If you have the recording, listen to the following dialogue. If you don't – read on.

You are trying to ask the way to the post office...

You   Signomi, poo ine to taxithromio parakalo?
Answer   To taxithromio then ine etho konda. *Ya va* to *vris* prepi *napas* sto *telostoothromookenaproxorisisya enamiliperipoo.* Eki *stripse* theksia ke ine konda se ena polikatastima *san* to Notos Galleries. Thexia ine ena ble magazi ke *apenandi* ine i trapeza. Eki ine to taxithromio!

Can you find your way with the key words? I think you'll get there!

▶ Good news grammar

1 Doing more things with verbs: the past

To talk about something that happened before or in the past in Greek, you need to change the verb. This happens in two stages: First you learn the pattern in Greek for *I did*, or *I went*, or *I could* and then you learn the pattern for the other verb endings. Remember the endings of the present tense? -o-ete/ite, -i, -oome and -oon(e)? For the past tense it's -a, -ate, -e, -ame and -an(e). Look at the pattern for 'buy':

I bought	agoras-a	*we bought*	agoras-ame
you bought	agoras-ate	*they bought*	agoras-ane
he/she/it bought	agoras-e		

Spend a couple of minutes on these every day until you know them in your sleep. If all fails stick them on the fridge!

Among the 30 **Instant** verbs there's one 'rebel', one that's different in the past tense. So you'd better learn it straight away:

I was	*you were*	*he/she/it was*	*we were*	*they were*
imoona	isaste	itan	imaste	itan(e)

Here are some more everyday verbs which you'll need both in the present and in the past – now you know how it's done.

I have	exo	*I had*	ixa
I do	kano	*I did*	ekana
I go	pao	*I went*	piga
I work	thoolevo	*I worked*	thoolepsa
I need	xriazome	*I needed*	xriastika
I can	boro	*I could*	boresa
I fix	ftiaxno	*I fixed*	eftiaksa
I eat	tro-o	*I ate*	efaga
I take	perno	*I took*	pira
I want	THelo	*I wanted*	iTHela
I think/believe	pistevo	*I thought*	pistepsa
I see	vlepo	*I saw*	itha

Phew! That's quite a list! Take a few minutes *every day* to learn these – don't try it in one go.

The ones starting with an e sometimes lose it along the line (ekana, but kanate), but don't worry about it.

2 *na* (to): makes sense

Prepi na pao: (*I must (to) go*). Boroome na pame (*we can (to) go*). So what is the **na** (to) doing there? Think of *must* as *have to* and of *can* as *are able to*… and it makes sense!

▶ Let's speak Greek

Over to you! Cover up the answers below. Always answer OUT LOUD! Start with a ten-point warm-up. Say in Greek:

1 Now we must go.
2 I want to do the shopping.
3 Are the shops open?
4 I am sorry, but it is very expensive.
5 Is there a bus for the centre?
6 We ate at the Taverna Aliki.
7 Can we buy wine at the supermarket?
8 It costs 130 euros.
9 We have been here from three to half past four.
10 Good grief, the wine was expensive!

Answer in Greek using **Oxi**. Speak about yourself.

11 Xriazeste mia mihani analipsis?
12 Exi pothosfero stin tileorasi?
13 Agorasate tipota sto farmakio?

Answer in Greek using the words in brackets.

14 Ti agorasate?   (tipota = *nothing*)
15 Pote piyenete (*go*) sto pothosfero?   (simera, stis thio)
16 Mexri pote ine anixta ta magazia?   (mexri tis eksi)
17 Pios efage para poli?   (Emis, fagame)
18 Poo ithate tin valitsa?   (itha, magazi)
19 Agorasate gramatosima etho?   (oxi, sto taxithromio)
20 Ti kero kani simera?   (kani krio, simera)

Answers

1 Tora prepi na pame.
2 THelo na kano ta psonia.
3 Ine ta magazia anixta?
4 Lipame, ala ine poli akrivo.
5 Exi leoforio ya to kendro?
6 Fagame stin taverna Aliki.
7 Boroome na agorasoome krasi sto soopermarket?
8 Kostizi ekato trianda evro.
9 Imaste etho apo tis tris mexri tis teseris ke misi.
10 THee moo, to krasi itan akrivo!
11 Oxi then xriazome mia mixani analipsis.

12 Oxi, then exi pothosfero stin tileorasi.
13 Oxi, then agorasa tipota sto farmakio.
14 Then agorasa tipota.
15 Piyeno sto pothosfero simera stis thio.
16 Ta magazia ine anixta mexri tis eksi.
17 Emis fagame para poli.
18 Itha tin valitsa se ena magazi.
19 Oxi, agorasa ta gramatosima sto taxithromio.
20 O keros ine kakos. Kani krio simera.

▶ Let's speak more Greek

For these optional exercises add an extra 15 minutes to your daily schedule. And remember, don't worry about getting the article or endings wrong. Near enough is good enough!

In your own words

This exercise will teach you to express yourself freely. Use only the words you have learned so far.

Tell me in your own words that...

1 you must go shopping today
2 you are aiming for the middle of the town
3 you want the bus
4 you have to go first to an ATM...
5 ...then you have to go to the pharmacy
6 you saw a supermarket but it was not open
7 you have to buy black shoes, size 37
8 you bought the shoes, they were a bit expensive
9 you did not buy much in the supermarket
10 you bought bread, a piece of cheese and a bottle of white wine

Answers

1 Prepi na pao ya psonia simera.
2 THelo na pao sto kendro.
3 THelo to leoforio.
4 Prepi na pao prota se mia mixani analipsis.
5 ...meta, prepi na pao sto farmakio.
6 Itha ena soopermarket, ala then itan anixto.
7 Prepi na agoraso mavra papootsia, noomero trianda epta.
8 Agorasa ta papootsia, ala itan ligo akriva.
9 Then agorasa pola pragmata sto soopermarket.
10 Agorasa psomi, ena komati tiri ke ena bookali aspro krasi.

▶ Let's speak Greek – fast and fluently

Translate each section and check if it is correct, then cover up the answers and say the three or four sentences fast!

20 seconds per section for a silver star, 15 seconds for a gold star.

Some of the English is in 'Greek-speak' to help you.

Excuse me, are you buying a television?
Is it expensive, the white television?
No, not too much. In England costs the same.

Signomi. Agorazete mia tileorasi?
Ine akrivi, i aspri tileorasi?
Oxi, oxi poli. Stin Anglia kostizi to ithio.

We would like to buy a suitcase.
We have a suitcase but it is too small.
I've seen a red suitcase but it is too expensive.

THeloome na agorasoome mia valitsa.
Exoome mia valitsa ala ine poli mikri.
Itha mia kokini valitsa ala ine poli akrivi.

The weather was bad in April.
I was in Volos. I ate in the town centre.
The restaurant was very expensive – 300 euros.
The waiter wasn't handsome but he was very nice.

O keros itan asximos ton Aprilio.
Imoona sto Volo. Efaga sto kendro.
To estiatorio itan poli akrivo – triakosia evro.
O servitoros then itan omorfos ala itan poli kalos.

Now say **all** the sentences in Greek without stopping and starting.

If you can do it in under one minute you are a fast and fluent winner!

But if you are not happy with your result – just try once more.

▶ Learn by heart

Say this dialogue in under a minute and with a lot of expression!

Pame ya psonia

Tom Simera kani krio. Exi pothosfero stin tileorasi.

Kate Lipame ala prepi na kanoome ta psonia. Then exoome tipota* na fame. Prepi na pame prota stin mixani analipsis, ke meta sto soopermarket.

(argotera)

Kate Etho ine ta psonia! Agorasa pola: zambon, tiri, psomi ke gramatosima ya tin Anglia.

Tom Kati ya mena? Oxi bira? Oxi krasi? Tipota ya mena? THee moo!

---

*tipota: *nothing*

Test your progress

Translate in writing. Then check your answers on page 88 and be amazed!

1 First I want to go to the cash dispenser.
2 In this the shop the shoes cost too much.
3 Did you see my husband in the chemist's?
4 We were here until a quarter past ten.
5 We saw the tennis in England on (in) television.
6 I am sorry, but we do not have the same in red, in size (number) 44.
7 This the shop is not cheap.
8 Who repaired my telephone? You?
9 Here is the department store. But it is not open.
10 Today we did not buy too many things. Only bread and half a kilo (of) butter.
11 I ate everything – eggs, apples, potatoes and a piece (of) cheese.
12 We must do the shopping. Is this the centre?
13 Yesterday I was in the office (firm) until nine o'clock.
14 The English newspapers cost a lot in Greece.
15 Is there a bus? No? It does not matter.
16 He was a very nice sales assistant.
17 What is this? Something for me?
18 Did she buy the bag near here or at Notos Galleries?
19 Everything was very expensive. Therefore I did not buy anything.
20 We need three kilos, I believe.

Remember the **Progress chart**? You are now halfway there!

04

week four

Study for 45 minutes a day – but if you are keen try 50 or 55!

Day one

- Read **Let's go and eat**.
- Listen to/Read **Pame na fame**.
- Listen to/Read the **New words**. Learn the easy ones.

Day two

- Repeat the dialogue. Learn the harder **New words**.
- Cut out the **Flash words** to help you.

Day three

- Learn all the **New words** until you know them well.
- Read and learn the **Good news grammar**.

Day four

- Listen to/Read **Learn by heart**.
- Cut out and learn the ten **Flash sentences**.

Day five

- Read **Say it simply**.
- Listen to/Read **Let's speak Greek**.

Day six

- Listen to/Read **Let's speak more Greek** (optional).
- Listen to/Read **Let's speak Greek – fast and fluently** (optional).
- Listen to/Read **Spot the keys**.
- Translate **Test your progress**.

Day seven

Are you keeping your scores above 60%? In that case...
have a good day off!

day-by-day guide

Let's go and eat

Tom and Kate are back in Athens. Pavlos Thiamandis invites them to dinner.

Kate   Tom, someone has telephoned. He did not say why. Mister Thiamandis from Thesaloniki. Here is the number.

Tom   Ah yes, Pavlos Thiamandis, a good client. His firm is in Thessaloniki. I know him well. He is very nice. I have an appointment with him on Thursday. It is important.

Tom   *(Telephones)* Hello! Good morning Mr Thiamandis. I am Tom Walker... Yes, thank you... yes, sure, it is possible... of course... next week, very interesting... no, we have time. Wonderful! No, only two days... ah yes... when? Tonight, at eight ... upstairs, by the exit... in front of the door. All right! In that case, until tonight, thank you very much, goodbye.

Kate   What are we doing tonight?

Tom   We are eating with Mr Thiamandis. In the centre, behind the church. He says that it is a new and very good restaurant. Mr Thiamandis is for three days in Athens with Edith and Peter Palmer from our company.

Kate   I know Edith Palmer. She is boring and thinks that she knows everything. She has a terrible dog. Well... I believe I am sick. I have a bad cold and pain. I need a doctor.

Tom   No, please! It's not possible! Mr Thiamandis is very important.

(At the restaurant) Anthreas, the head waiter, explains the menu.

Anthreas The fish is not on the menu and for dessert today there is baklavas or ice cream.

Pavlos   Mrs Walker, can I help you? Perhaps a suvlaki and afterwards a salad?

Kate   A steak with salad, please.

Edith   A steak, Kate? It is too much red meat.

Pavlos   And you, Mr Walker, what would you like? And what do you want to drink?

Tom   A large suvlaki with chips and vegetables and a beer, please.

Edith   The vegetables have a lot of oil, Tom. ⸱⸱⸱⸱➡ Page 52

▶ Pame na fame

Tom and Kate are back in Athens. Pavlos Thiamandis invites them to dinner.

Kate   Tom, kapios tilefonise. Then ipe yati. O kirios Thiamandis apo tin THesaloniki. Etho ine to noomero.

Tom   Ah, ne, o Pavlos Thiamandis, enas kalos pelatis. I eteria too ine stin THesaloniki. Ton ksero kala. Ine poli kalos. Exo ena randevoo mazi too tin Pempti. Ine simandiko.

Tom   *(Tilefoni)* Parakalo! Kalimera, kirie Thiamandi. Ime o Tom Walker... Ne, efxaristo... ne, vevea, ine thinaton... fisika... tin epomeni evthomatha, poli enthiaferon... oxi, exoome kero. Eksoxa! Oxi, mono thio meres... ah ne... pote? Apopse, stis okto... epano, thipla stin eksotho... brosta stin porta. Endaksi! Etsi, apopse, efxaristo poli, adio.

Kate   Ti kanoome apopse?

Tom   Trome me ton kirio Thiamandi. Sto kendro, piso apo tin eklisia. Lei oti ine kenooryio ke ena poli kalo estiatorio. O kirios Thiamandis ine ya tris meres stin ATHina me tin Edith ke ton Peter Palmer apo tin eteria mas.

Kate   Ksero tin Edith Palmer. Ine vareti ke pistevi oti ta kseri ola. Exi enan apesio skilo. Lipon... pistevo oti ime arosti. Exo ena kako krioma ke pono. Xriazome enan yatro.

Tom   Oxi, se parakalo! Then ine thinaton! O kirios Thiamandis ine poli simandikos.

(Sto estiatorio) Anthreas, the head waiter, explains the menu.

Anthreas To psari then ine sto menoo ke ya epithorpio exoome simera baklava i pagoto.

Pavlos   Kiria Walker, boro na sas voiTHiso? Isos ena soovlaki ke meta mia salata?

Kate   Mia brizola me salata, parakalo.

Edith   Brizola, Kate? Para poli kokino kreas.

Pavlos   Ke esis, kirie Walker, ti THelete? Ke ti THelete na pyite.

Tom   Ena megalo soovlaki me patates tiganites ke laxanika ke mia bira, parakalo.

Edith   Ta laxanika exoone poli lathi, Tom.

······▶ Page 53

Pavlos	And you, Mrs Palmer?
Edith	I want a little grilled chicken and a glass of water, please.
(Later)	
Pavlos	Do we want fruit, or perhaps something better – the baklava? No? Nothing? Have we finished? A coffee for someone? Nobody? Well... It is late. The bill, please.
Edith	Mr Thiamandis, can you help me please? How do they say 'doggy bag' in Greek? I want a little meat for my dog.
Kate	But Edith, the dog is in England!

▶ New words

kapios, kapion *someone*
tilefonise *(has) telephoned*
ipe *he/she/it said*
yati *why*
pelatis *client*
ksero *I know*
kala *well*
randevoo *appointment*
mazi too *with him*
Pempti *Thursday*
simandiko *important*
parakalo *not at all (and what you say when answering the phone)*
efxaristo/efxaristo poli *thank you/thank you very much*
thinaton *possible*
fisika *of course/naturally*
tin epomeni evthomatha *next week*
enthiaferon, enthiaferoossa *interesting*
kero *time*
eksoxa *wonderful*
apopse *tonight*
epano *up/upstairs*
thipla *by, next to*

eksothos *exit*
brosta *in front of*
porta *door*
endaksi *all right, OK*
trome *we eat*
piso apo *behind*
eklisia *church*
lei *he/she says*
oti *that*
estiatorio *restaurant*
mas *our*
pistevi *he/she/it believes*
kseri *he/she/it knows*
apesio *terrible*
skilos *dog*
arostos/i *sick*
krioma *cold/flu*
pono *pain*
yatros *doctor*
psari *fish*
menoo *menu*
epithorpio *dessert*
baklavas *famous Greek pastry*
pagoto *ice cream*
voiTHiso *to help*
soovlaki *Greek meat dish (like shish kebab)*

Pavlos	Ke esis, kiria Palmer?
Edith	THelo kotopoolo psito ke ena potiri nero, parakalo.
(Argotera)	
Pavlos	THeloome froota, i isos kati kalitero – baklava? Oxi? Tipota? Teliosame? Kafe ya kapion? Kanis? Lipon... ine arga. Ton logariasmo, parakalo.
Edith	Kirie Thiamandi, borite na me voiTHisete, parakalo? Pos lene 'doggy bag' sta Elinika? THelo ligo kreas ya ton skilo moo.
Kate	Ma Edith, o skilos ine stin Anglia!

salata	*salad*	nero	*water*
kreas	*meat*	froota	*fruit*
brizola	*steak*	teliosame	*we've finished/ we finished*
(na) pyite	*to drink*		
patates tiganites	*chips*	kanis	*nobody/anyone*
laxanika	*vegetables*	arga	*late; slow(ly)*
lathi	*oil*	borite na me voiTHisete	*can you help me?*
kotopoolo	*chicken*		
psito	*grilled*	Pos lene sta Elinika ...	*How do you say in Greek ...?*
potiri	*glass*		

TOTAL NEW WORDS: 65
...only 92 words to go!

Last easy extras

Days of the week – *meres tis evthomathas*

Theftera	*Monday*	Paraskevi	*Friday*
Triti	*Tuesday*	Savato	*Saturday*
Tetarti	*Wednesday*	Kiriaki	*Sunday*
Pempti	*Thursday*		

▶ Good news grammar

1 Verbs again

Here are the new verbs that appeared in the dialogue in Week 4. Once again I'll give you both the present and the past as the base for your mental acrobatics.

I say	leo*	*I said*	ipa
I know	ksero	*I knew*	iksera
I help	voiTHo	*I helped*	voiTHisa
I phone	tilefono	*I phoned*	tilefonisa

*leo is a rebel. Look him up on page 81 and shudder.

Four pairs – eight minutes to learn. And then you can say a whole lot more, such as – what you said, whom you phoned, and what you knew… Go for it!

And more good news, if you ever get confused or forget: there's a complete summary of verbs in Week 6 **Good news grammar**. Have a sneak preview! You'll know most of these in three weeks' time!

And if all else fails you can always say 'Pos lene sta Elinika…?' And everyone will be rushing to help.

2 'it', 'her', 'him' and 'them'

Imagine you're talking about certain things – wine, the company, holidays or seats on the plane, or certain people – Tom, Kate, a client. Now imagine you are just referring to these things, or people without actually saying their name. You would say *it* or *them*.

In Greek *it*, *her*, *him* are **ton**, **tin**, **to** and *them* is **tous**, **tis**, **ta**, depending on the word you are referring to.

Agorazo to krasi →	to agorazo	(*I buy it*)
Agorazo tin bira →	tin agorazo	(*I buy it*)
Agorazo ta papootsia →	ta agorazo	(*I buy them*)
Ksero tous yatri →	tous ksero	(*I know them*)
Ksero ta spitia →	ta ksero	(*I know them*)

Did you notice? The *it* or *them* always goes in front of the verb; *It I buy, It you buy, Them we know.*

3 'think' and 'know'

Here are two more everyday verbs which deserve some extra attention. By now you know the sequence: it's always *I – you – he/she/it – we – they*. So this time the gift boxes are quite thin:

know: **ksero**

now:	ksero	kserete	kseri	kseroome	kseroon(e)
yesterday:	iksera	kserate	iksere	kserame	kseran(e)

think/believe: **pistevo**

today		last year	
pistevo	pistevoome	pistepsa	pistepsame
pistevete	pistevoon(e)	pistepsate	pistepsan(e)
pistevi		pistepse	

4 Attention!

Here's something unusual and different from other languages: when you want to say in Greek *he can go* you actually say: *he can goes* – **bori na pai**. When the two verbs come together: *able to + go* or *want to + go*, note they both take the same ending.

Boroome na pame. THelo na pao.

5 Best news: *prepi na* – must/have to

Prepi na never changes: no endings to learn! *I must, you must, we must…* It's always **prepi na**. If you want to make sure *who must* you can add the person: ego, emis, esis, etc…. easy!

▶ Learn by heart

Here is a short piece about someone who is rather fed up. Put yourself in his shoes. Learn it and act it out in under 50 seconds.

> **A** Kserete ton kirio Andoni? Tilefonise tora. THeli na fao mazi too.
> **B** Yati?
> **A** Ine enas simandikos pelatis. Mono poo then ine kalos. Troi ke pini para poli.
> **B** Ke pote?
> **A** Apopse! Exi pothosfero stin tileorasi. THelo na po* oti ime arostos ala then boro… panda** i eteria! THee moo!
> **B** Aah… Lipame.

*po: *say* **panda: *always*

Say it simply

When people want to speak Greek but don't dare, it's usually because they are trying to translate what they want to say from English into Greek. And because they don't know some of the words they give up!

With **Instant Greek** you work around the words you don't know with the words you do know! And believe me, 370 words are enough to say anything! It may not always be very elegant, but who cares? You are speaking and communicating!

Here are three examples, showing you how to say things in a simple way. The English words which are not part of the **Instant** vocabulary are in **bold**.

1 You need to **change your flight** to London from Tuesday to Friday.

This is what you could say – simply:

THelo na paro to aeroplano ya to Lonthino tin Paraskevi, oxi tin Triti.

2 You want to get your **purse** and **mobile phone** from the **coach** which the driver has locked.

Say it simply:

Signomi. Prepi na paro ta xrimata moo ke to kinito moo apo to leoforio.

3 This time your friend has **broken the heel** of her **only pair of** shoes. You have to **catch** a plane and need some help now.

This is what you could say:

Signomi, ta papootsia tis filis moo then ine endaksi.
Prepi na ta ftiaksoome ke na pame sto aeroplano. Xriazome voiTHia tora.

▶ Let's speak Greek

Here are eight sentences to say in Greek, and then on to greater things!

1 I am sorry, I do not have time.
2 Are we going with him?
3 I want (would like) a salad.
4 We were here yesterday.
5 Excuse me, what did you say?
6 I did not take it.
7 When did you work in Greece?
8 We did not do anything.

Now pretend you are in Greece with English friends who do not speak Greek. They will want you to ask someone something and will want you to do it for them in Greek. They will say: 'Please ask him...'. Start with **Signomi**...

9 if he knows Mr Thiamandis.
10 where he bought the stamps.
11 if he has an appointment now.
12 where the restaurant is.

Now your friends will ask you to tell someone something. They use some words which you don't know, so you have to use **Instant** words. They will say: 'Please tell her that...'. Start your sentence with **Lipame**...

13 her suvlaki is cold.
14 we are having only water, no wine.
15 she is a vegetarian.
16 he does not have the number.

While shopping you are offered various items. You take them all, saying 'yes, I take it' using the right form of 'it'.

17 ta fro**o**ta?
18 to pago**to**?

19 tin b**i**ra?
20 ton ka**fe**?

Answers

1 Lipame, then **e**xo ker**o**.
2 Pame maz**i** too?
3 TH**e**lo m**i**a sal**a**ta.
4 **I**maste eth**o** xTH**e**s.
5 Signomi, ti **i**pate?
6 Then to p**i**ra.
7 P**o**te thool**e**psate stin El**a**tha?
8 Then k**a**name t**i**pota.
9 Signomi, ks**e**rete ton k**i**rio Thiam**a**ndi?
10 Signomi, poo agor**a**sate ta gramat**o**sima?

11 Signomi, **e**xete **e**na randev**oo** t**o**ra?
12 Signomi, poo **i**ne to estiat**o**rio?
13 Lipame, to soovl**a**ki tis **i**ne kr**i**o.
14 Lipame, ex**oo**me m**o**no ner**o**, **o**xi kras**i**.
15 Lipame, then tr**o**i kr**e**as.
16 Lipame, then **e**xi to n**o**omero.
17 Ne, ta p**e**rno.
18 Ne, to p**e**rno.
19 Ne, tin p**e**rno.
20 Ne, ton p**e**rno.

▶ Let's speak more Greek

In your own words

This exercise will teach you to express yourself freely. Use only the words you have learned so far.

Tell me in your own words that...

1 somebody telephoned – it was Pavlos
2 you have an appointment with him next week
3 he works for a firm in Athens
4 he is a good client
5 you're going to eat in a new restaurant
6 you've got a bad cold – you need a doctor
7 you don't have time to go to the doctor
8 you can go to the chemist
9 you'd like a steak with potatoes and salad
10 you went home at half past eleven

Answers

1 Kapios tilefonise – itan o Pavlos.
2 Exo randevoo mazi too tin epomeni evthomatha.
3 Thoolevi ya mia eteria stin ATHina.
4 Ine kalos pelatis.
5 Trome se ena kenoorio estiatorio.
6 Exo ena asximo krioma – xriazome enan yatro.
7 Then exo kero na pao sto yatro.
8 Boro na pao sto farmakio.
9 THelo mia brizola me patates ke mia salata.
10 Piga sto spiti stis entheka ke misi.

▶ Let's speak Greek – fast and fluently

Translate each section and check if it is correct, then cover up the answers and say the three or four sentences fast!

20 seconds per section for a silver star, 15 seconds for a gold star.

Some of the English is in 'Greek-speak' to help you.

Do you know Ari Thiamandis? He phoned yesterday.
Why? He said it was important.
The appointment in Athens was on Wednesday.

*Kserete ton **A**ri Thiamand**i**? Tilef**o**nise xTHes.*
*Yat**í**? **I**pe **o**ti **i**tan simandik**o**.*
*To randev**oo** stin ATHina **i**tan tin Tetarti.*

Ari is in Athens for three days.
There is a restaurant behind the church.
Ari says it's very good.

*O **A**ris **i**ne stin ATHina ya tris m**e**res.*
***E**xi **e**na estiat**o**rio pis**o** ap**o** tin eklis**i**a.*
*O **A**ris l**e**i **o**ti **i**ne pol**í** kal**o**.*

Unfortunately, I can't go to the restaurant.
My dog is ill. He has eaten too much meat.
Oh, I am very sorry. How do you say in Greek: 'Poor little thing?' (o kaimenos)

*Thistix**o**s, then bor**o** na p**a**o sto estiat**o**rio.*
*O sk**í**los moo **i**ne arostos. **E**faye para pol**í** kreas.*
*O, lip**a**me pol**í**. Pos l**e**ne sta Elinik**a**: 'Poor little thing'? O kaim**e**nos.*

Now say **all** the sentences in Greek without stopping and starting.

If you can do it in under one minute you are a fast and fluent winner!

But if you are not happy with your result – just try once more.

▶ Spot the keys

You practised listening for key words when you asked the way to the post office in Week 3. Now you are in a department store. You have asked the sales assistant if the black dress you liked is also available in size 44. She said: 'Oxi, mia stigmi, parakalo...' and disappeared. When she came back this is what she said:

Thistixos exoome noomero saranda tesera mono se prasino. *Then exoome kanena mavro forema se gfto to meyeTHos.* Ala exoome *mavra foremata* se noomero saranda thio *yati poli pelates zitoone gfto* to *meyeTHos.* To noomero saranda thio *mavro pistevo,* ine arketa megalo *ya sas.*

It appears that size 44 was only available in green but she believes that size 42 might be big enough.

Test your progress

Translate in writing. Then check your answers on page 88.

1 Has someone telephoned Mr Thiamandis?
2 I want to know where the restaurant is.
3 It is late and he is not there. What are we doing tonight?
4 Here is the menu! Do you know the wines of Ahaia?
5 The cash dispenser is upstairs, behind the exit, near the door.
6 Wednesday we must go to the doctor. It is an important appointment.
7 Why do I say she is boring? Because I know her well.
8 Did you see him? I must go to Larisa with him.
9 Mr Thiamandis is my client. He has bought everything.
10 I want to buy this thing. How does one say in Greek...?
11 Next week? I am sorry. It is not possible.
12 Can you help me please? Many thanks!
13 Three hundred euros for two days. Very interesting. Yes, of course we take it.
14 I must buy three things for my friends.
15 I have a cold. I need a doctor.
16 Can they eat only the baklava?
17 There is a terrible dog. What can we do?
18 Nobody saw who ate the steak.
19 Can I say something: the chicken is not bad but the fish is better.
20 What do you take? The fruit? Yes, sure, it is from Ahaia.

How are your 'shares' looking on the **Progress chart**? Going up?

05

week five

How about 15 minutes on the train, tube or bus, 10 minutes on the way home and 20 minutes before switching on the television...?

Day one

- Read **On the move**.
- Listen to/Read **Taksithevondas**.
- Listen to/Read the **New words**. Learn 15 or more.

Day two

- Repeat the dialogue. Learn the harder **New words**.
- Cut out the **Flash words** to get stuck in.

Day three

- Test yourself to perfection on all the **New words**.
- Read and learn the **Good news grammar**.

Day four (the tough day)

- Listen to/Read **Learn by heart**.
- Cut out and learn the ten **Flash sentences**.

Day five

- Listen to/Read **Let's speak Greek**.
- Go over **Learn by heart**.

Day six

- Listen to/Read **Let's speak more Greek** (optional).
- Listen to/Read **Let's speak Greek – fast and fluently** (optional).
- Listen to/Read **Spot the keys**.
- Translate **Test your progress**.

Day seven

I bet you don't want a day off... but I insist!

day-by-day guide

On the move

Tom and Kate are travelling through Southern Greece – by train, bus and hire car. They talk to Anna, the ticket clerk at the station, to Jim on the train and later to Antonis, the bus driver.

At the station

Tom	Two tickets for Patras, please.
Anna	Withreturn?
Tom	With what? Can you speak more slowly, please?
Anna	With–return?
Tom	No, one way only. What time is there a train and from which platform?
Anna	At ten minutes to four. Platform eight.
Kate	Quickly, Tom, here are two seats, non-smoking. Oh, but someone is smoking. Excuse me, you cannot smoke, because it is non-smoking here. It is forbidden to smoke.
Jim	I am sorry. I don't understand, I speak only English.

At the bus stop

Kate	There is no bus. We have to wait 20 minutes. Tom, here are my postcards. Over there is a letter-box. I want to take some photos. The town is beautiful in the sun.
Tom	Kate, come on! There are a lot of people. Here are two buses! Both are blue. This one is full. Let's take the other one. (*on the bus*) Two for Sparti, please.
Antonis	This bus goes only to Corinth.
Tom	But we are in Corinth!
Antonis	Yes, yes, but this is the bus for the hospital of Corinth.

In the car

Tom	Here is our car. Only 120 euros for three days. I am very satisfied.
Kate	I do not like the car. It costs so little because it's very old. Let's hope that we don't have problems.
Tom	I am sorry. The first car was too expensive and the second (one) too big. This was the last one.
	(*Later*) Where are we? There is no map! On the left there is a petrol station, and on the right there is a school. Hurry up!

⋯⟶ Page 66

▶ Taksithevondas

Tom and Kate are travelling through Southern Greece – by train, bus and hire car. They talk to Anna, the ticket clerk at the station, to Jim on the train and later to Antonis, the bus driver.

Ston stathmo

Tom	Thio isitiria ya tin Patra, parakalo.
Anna	Me-epistrofi?
Tom	Me ti? Borite na milisete pio arga, parakalo?
Anna	Me epistrofi?
Tom	Oxi, mono mias katefTHinsis. Ti ora exi treno ke apo pia platforma?
Anna	Stis tesseris para theka. Platforma okto.
Kate	Grigora Tom, etho ine thio THesis, ya mi kapnizondes. Ah, ala kapios kapnizi. Signomi, then borite na kapnisete, ine ya mi kapnizondes etho. Apagorevete to kapnisma.
Jim	Sorry, I don't understand, milao only Anglika.

Stin stasi leoforiou

Kate	Then exi leoforio. Prepi na perimenoome ikosi lepta. Tom, etho ine ta kart-postal moo. Eki pera ine ena gramatokivotio. THelo na paro merikes fotografies. I poli ine poli omorfi ston ilio.
Tom	Kate, ela! Exi poli kosmo. Etho ine thio leoforia! Ke ta thio ine ble. Afto ine yemato. As paroome to alo.
	(sto leoforio) Thio ya Sparti, parakalo.
Antonis	Afto to leoforio pai mono stin KorinTHo.
Tom	Ala imaste stin KorinTHo!
Antonis	Ne, ne, ala afto ine to leoforio ya to nosokomio tis KorintTHoo.

Sto aftokinito

Tom	Etho ine to aftokinito mas. Mono ekatoikosi evro ya tris meres. Ime poli ikanopioimenos.
Kate	Then moo aresi to aftokinito. Kostizi toso ligo yati ine poli palio. As elpisoome oti then THa exoome kanena provlima.
Tom	Lipame. To proto aftokinito itan poli akrivo ke to theftero poli megalo. Afto itan to telefteo.
	(Argotera) Poo imaste? Then exi xarti! Aristera ine ena venzinathiko ke theksia ine ena skolio. Kane grigora!

••••➡ Page 67

Kate   We are coming from the underground station. The main road is at the (traffic) lights. It's perhaps three kilometres until the motorway. *(On the motorway)* Why does the car go slowly? Have we enough petrol? How many litres? Do we have oil? Is the engine too hot? They gave us a wreck. Where is the mobile phone? Where is the number of the garage? Where is my bag?

Tom   Kate, please! I have a headache. And now it's raining! And why are the police behind us?

▶ New words

taksithevondas *on the move/ travelling*

staTHmos *(railway) station*

isitirio *ticket*

me epistrofi *(with) return*

mias katefTHinsis *one way*

borite na milisete …? *can you speak …?*

pio *more*

treno *train*

pios, pia, pio *who, which*

platforma *platform*

grigora *quickly*

mi kapnizondes *non-smoking*

kapnizi *he/she/it smokes*

apagorevete to kapnisma *it's forbidden to smoke*

then katalaveno *I don't understand*

milao *I speak*

stasi *(bus) stop*

perimeno *I wait*

kart-postal *postcard*

eki pera *over there*

gramatokivotio *letter-box*

fotografia *photograph*

poli *city/town*

ilios *the sun*

exi kosmo *it's crowded*

ke ta thio *both (and the two)*

yematos/i/o *full*

alo *other*

nosokomio *hospital*

aftokinito *car*

mera, meres *day, days*

ikanopioimenos/i/o *satisfied, happy*

moo aresi/then moo aresi *I like/I don't like*

palios/ia/io *old (things)*

as elpisume *let's hope*

then THa exoome *we won't have*

provlima *problem*

proto *first,* theftero *second,* telefteo *last*

xartis, xarti *map*

venzinathiko *petrol station*

skolio *school*

kane grigora! *hurry up!*

erxomaste *we come/we're coming*

ipoyio *underground*

kendrikos thromos *main road (central road)*

fanaria *lights (also used for traffic lights)*

xiliometro *kilometre*

aftokinitothromos *motorway*

venzini *petrol*

posi, poses, posa *how many*

litro *litre*

mixani *machine/engine*

zesti *hot*

saravalo *wreck*

Kate   Erxomaste apo ton ipoyio. O kendrikos thromos ine sta fanaria. Ine isos tria xiliometra mexri ton aftokinitothromo. *(Ston aftokinitothromo)* Yati pai to aftokinito arga? **E**xoome arketi venzini? **P**osa litra? **E**xoome lathi? **I**ne i mixani poli zesti? Mas ethosan ena saravalo. Poo ine to kinito tilefono? Poo ine to noomero too garaz? Poo ine i tsanda moo?

Tom   Kate, se parakalo! **E**xo ponokefalo. Ke tora vrexi! Ke yati ine i astinomia piso mas?

garaz *garage (car mechanic's garage)*	ponokefalo *headache*
tsanda *bag*	vroxi *rain* (vrexi – *it's raining*)
	astinomia *police*

TOTAL NEW WORDS: 59
...only 33 words to go!

▶ Learn by heart

Someone has pranged the car and someone else is getting suspicious! Try to say these lines fluently and like a prize-winning play!

Pame ya tenis

A   Pame ya tenis.
Moo aresoon i thio Amerikani.
Exo isitiria apo tin eteria moo.
As paroome to leoforio i kalitera pame me ton ipoyio.
Exi treno oli tin imera.

B   Me to leoforio? Ton ipoyio? To treno? Yati?
Ti simveni?*
Exoome ena aftokinito eki kato.

A   Eh... xTHes, me tin vroxi then itha ta fanaria. Then ine tipota, mono i porta ke o mixanikos sto garaz itan poli kalos!

---

*Ti simveni?: *What's the matter?*

▶ Good news grammar

1 *moo, sas, too, tis... (e)mena, (e)sena, afton, aftin*

Learning these cold is difficult, but when they come up in the text or the **Flash cards** it's not so bad. Here's the first team:

moo	sas	too	tis	mas	tus
my	*your*	*his*	*her*	*our*	*their*

The second team gives you some useful combinations. Spend five minutes learning them and take another five minutes to remember.

ya mena	ya sas (sena)	ya afton	ya aftin	ya mas	ya aftoos
for me	*for you*	*for him*	*for her*	*for us*	*for them*

You use the same words with apo (*from*) and mazi me (*with*).

2 Last handful of verbs

Week 5 verbs – neatly lined up for easy learning. Ten minutes will do it.

I speak	milao	*I spoke*	milisa
I smoke	kapnizo	*I smoked*	kapnisa
I wait	perimeno	*I waited*	perimena
I like	moo aresi/moo aresoon(e)	*I liked*	moo arese/aresan
I give	thino	*I gave*	ethosa

3 last giftbox... *erxome* (come)

Erxome is a rebel! Five minutes while you're grooming the dog.

	I	you	he/she/it	we	they
tora:	erxome	erxosaste	erxete	erxomaste	erxode
xthes:	ilTHa	ilTHate	ilTHe	ilTHame	ilTHan(e)

4 *Moo aresi/then moo aresi* (I like/I don't like)

You will use this all the time. Think how often you use *I like – I don't like* in English! Unfortunately it needs a bit of mental acrobatics, because in Greek *I like* is literally *it pleases me*: moo (*me*) aresi (*it pleases*). *I don't like* is: then moo aresi, then moo aresi to Internet (*I don't like the internet*).

If several things please you it's 'moo aresoon'. Example: *I like the children* – moo aresoon ta pethia. And if *you, he* or *she, we* or *they like* something it would be: **sas** aresi, **too** or **tis** aresi, **mas** aresi or **toos** aresi. So you have to rethink it quickly until it's as automatic as changing gear. Then: sas aresi o Tom Cruise? – Ne, ne!

▶ Let's speak Greek

A ten-point warm-up: I give you an answer and you ask me a question as if you did not hear the words in CAPITAL LETTERS very well.

Example: O Nikos ine STO TAXITHROMIO. Poo ine o Nikos?

1 Ena tilefono ya TIN ELENI SOFIANOO.
2 Imoona sto nosokomio TON MARTIO.
3 O Tom THeli na milisi ME TON KIRIO THIAMANDI.
4 To isitirio me epistrofi ya tin ATHina kostizi EKSINDATRIA EVRO.
5 Then exume kero ya ta FANARIA!
6 NE, ime ikanopioimenos me to spiti.
7 APAGOREVETE to kapnisma etho.
8 Pao stin Anglia ME TI FERRARI MOO.
9 Then ime ikanopioimenos me to spiti yati EXI POLA PROVLIMATA.
10 I thiakopes moo itan POLI KALES.

Answer in Greek using 'yes' or 'no'. Speak about yourself.

11 Exete venzini?
12 Erxete to treno?
13 Piyenete ston staTHmo?
14 Piyenete stin Larisa?
15 Kapnizete poli?

Explain these words in Greek. Your answers can vary from mine.

16 an au pair
17 kennel
18 a teacher
19 unemployed
20 to be broke

Answers

1 Ya pion ine to tilefono?
2 Pote minate sto nosokomio?
3 Se pion THeli na milisi o Tom?
4 Poso kostizi to isitirio me epistrofi ya tin ATHina?
5 Exoome kero ya ta fanaria?
6 Ise ikanopioimenos me to spiti?
7 Yati then boroome na kapnisoome.
8 Pos pate stin Anglia?
9 Yati then iste ikanopioimenos me to spiti?
10 Pos itan i thiakopes soo?
11 Ne, exo venzini.
12 Oxi, then erxete to treno.
13 Oxi, then piyeno ston staTHmo.
14 Ne, piyeno stin Larisa.
15 Oxi, then kapnizo poli.
16 Kapia poo voithai sto spiti.
17 Mikro spiti ya skiloos.
18 Kapios poo thoolevi sto skolio.
19 Kapios poo then exi thoolia.
20 Otan then exete lefta.

▶ Let's speak more Greek

In your own words

This exercise will teach you to express yourself freely. Use only the words you have learned so far.

Tell me in your own words that...

1 you bought a return ticket to Thessaloniki
2 there is a train at 10.15 from platform eight
3 it is not allowed, but somebody is smoking
4 on Monday you would like to go to Corinth (Korinthos) by bus
5 you must take some photos for your children
6 this bus is full; suggest that you take the other one
7 your car is cheap because it is very old
8 it is only 80 euros for four days
9 the car goes so slowly and the engine overheats
10 hopefully you won't have problems

Answers

1 Agorasa ena isitirio ya tin THesaloniki me epistrofi.
2 Exi ena treno stis theka ke tetarto apo tin platforma okto.
3 Apagorevete, ala kapios kapnizi.
4 Tin theftera THelo na pao stin KorinTHo me to leoforio.
5 Prepi na paro merikes fotografies ya ta pethia.
6 Afto to leoforio ine yemato. As paroome to alo.
7 To aftokinito moo ine ftino yati ine poli palio.
8 Ine mono ogthonda evro ya teseris meres.
9 To aftokinito pai toso arga, ke i mixani ine poli zesti.
10 Elpizo oti then THa exo/exoome kanena provlima.

▶ Let's speak Greek – fast and fluently

Translate each section and check if it is correct, then cover up the answers and say the three or four sentences fast!

25 seconds per section for a silver star, 20 seconds for a gold star.

Some of the English is in 'Greek-speak' to help you.

A ticket to Piraeus, please, only one way.
How much? €21? Can you speak more slowly, please?
Thank you. What time is the train?

Ena isitirio ya ton Pirea, parakalo, mono aplo.
Poso? Ikosiena evro? Borite na milisete pio arga, parakalo?
Efxaristo. Ti ora ine to treno?

We would like to take the bus.
We have to wait fifteen minutes.
We can take a photo.

THeloome na paroome to leoforio.
Prepi na perimenoome thekapende lepta.
Boroome na paroome mia fotografia.

We don't have a map of Greece (Elatha).
It's ten kilometres to the motorway.
The traffic lights are red.
We have a problem. Perhaps the car is broken (xalasmeno).
My wife has a headache.

Then exoome ena xarti tis Elathos.
Ine theka xiliometra mexri ton aftokinitothromo.
Ta fanaria ine kokina.
Exoome ena provlima. Isos to aftokinito ine xalasmeno.
I yineka moo exi ponokefalo.

Now say **all** the sentences in Greek without stopping and starting.

If you can do it in under one minute you are a fast and fluent winner!

▶ Spot the keys

This time you plan a trip in the country and wonder about the weather.

You Signomi, kserete ti kero kani avrio?

Answer Lipame, then ksero *ti kero kani* apo tin tileorasi *ala thiavasa stin efimeritha* oti o keros *THa ine astatos*. Apopse THa kani krio ke vroxi. *I THermocrasia* ine thekapende *vaTHmi* Kelsiou *ke tha exi THinato anemo*.

He doesn't know … something on television then you heard the word 'weather' and that it's going to be cold tonight and rainy. There's also something about 15 degrees Celsius, so you'd better take a jacket and an umbrella.

Test your progress

Translate in writing. Then check your answers and be amazed.

1 It is forbidden to go to the restaurant without shoes.
2 I like your Porsche. Was it very cheap?
3 When I am on holiday I always speak a lot of Greek.
4 I need six tickets. Do you have non-smoking seats?
5 I think that we have problems with the engine.
6 I do not like the Internet. It's very difficult.
7 I do not understand. Can you speak more slowly, please?
8 It's hot and it's crowded. Let's go to the town.
9 One hour with her gives me a headache.
10 There is a bus at the traffic lights. Where's it going?
11 The credit card isn't here. We have to telephone the police.
12 Let's do it like this: first we buy the Ferrari for me and afterwards the T-shirt for you.
13 I like this car, but the other (one) was better.
14 We have only one litre of petrol and there isn't (hasn't) a petrol station until Athens.
15 I like the sun and I like the rain. I like both.
16 (*On the phone*) Hello, we're 20 km from Athens. Is (has) there any garage?
17 Excuse me. I need help, please. I do not know Athens. Where is the station?
18 The main road? It's not too difficult. You take the metro.
19 Where are they? What did they do? I do not like to wait.
20 We are coming from (the) platform 17? Where is Spiros?

06

week six

This is your last week! Need I say more?

Day one

- Read **At the airport**.
- Listen to/Read **Sto aerothromio**.
- Listen to/Read the **New words**. There are only a handful!

Day two

- Read **Sto aerothromio**. Learn all the **New words**.
- Work with the **Flash words** and **Flash sentences**.

Day three

- Test yourself on the **Flash sentences**.
- Listen to/Read **Learn by heart**.

Day four

- No more **Good news grammar!** Have a look at the summary.
- Read **Say it simply**.

Day five

- Listen to/Read **Let's speak Greek**.
- Listen to/Read **Spot the keys**.

Day six

- Listen to/Read **Let's speak more Greek** (optional).
- Listen to/Read **Let's speak Greek – fast and fluently** (optional).
- Your last **Test your progress!** Go for it!

Day seven

Congratulations!

You have successfully completed the course and can now speak

Instant Greek!

---

day-by-day guide

At the airport

Tom and Kate are on their way home to Birmingham. They are in the departure lounge at Athens airport.

Tom On Monday we must work. Terrible! I would prefer to go to Miami or Honolulu. Nobody knows where I am and the office can wait.

Kate And *my* company? What do they do? They speak with my mother! She has the number of my mobile. And then?

Tom Yes, yes, I know (it). Well, perhaps at Christmas we can go for a week in the snow or to Madeira on a ship... There is a kiosk down there. I'll go and buy a newspaper... Kate! There is Aristotelis Nikou!

Ari Hello, how are you? What are you doing here? This is my wife, Nancy. Are the holidays over? How were they?

Kate Greece is wonderful. We saw a lot and ate too much. We know Ahaia and Skiathos very well now.

Ari Next year Thessaloniki! What a fantastic city!... Mrs Walker, my wife would like to buy a book about computers. Can you go with her to help her, please. Mr Walker, you have a newspaper. Are there any photos of the football? And afterwards are we going to drink something?

(At the kiosk)

Kate There is nothing here. I do not see anything interesting. Are you also going to England?

Nancy No, we are going to Sparti to Ari's mother. Our children are often with her in the holidays. Tomorrow we'll take the train. It costs less.

Kate Your husband works at the Bank of Greece?

Nancy Yes. The work is interesting, but the money is little. We have an apartment, but it is small, and an old car. You always need a lot of work. My family lives in California and my girlfriend is in Florida and we write a lot of letters. I would like to go to America but it is too expensive.

••••➤ Page 78

▶ Sto aerothromio

Tom and Kate are on their way home to Birmingham. They are in the departure lounge at Athens airport.

Tom Tin Theftera prepi na thoolepsoome. Apesio! Protimo na pame sto Miami i stin Xonolooloo. Kanis then kseri poo ime ke i eteria bori na perimeni.

Kate Ke i eteria moo? Ti kanoone? Milane stin mitera moo. Afti exi to noomero too kinitoo tilefonoo moo. Ke tote?

Tom Ne, ne, to ksero. Lipon, isos ta Xristooyena boroome na pame ya mia evthomatha sto xioni i stin Madeira me karavi... Ine ena periptero eki kato. Pao na agoraso mia efimeritha... Kate! O Aristotelis Nikou!

Ari Yasas, ti kanete? Ti kanete etho? Afti ine i yineka moo, i Nancy. I thiakopes teliosan? Pos itan?

Kate I Elatha ine iperoxi. Ithame pola pragmata ke fagame para poli. Kseroome tin Axaya ke tin SkiaTHo poli kala tora.

Ari Too xronoo i THesaloniki! Ti fandastiki poli!... Kiria Walker, i yineka moo THeli na agorasi ena vivlio ya komputer. Borite na pate mazi tis na tin voiTHisete, parakalo? Kirie Walker, exete mia efimeritha. Exi kamia fotografia pothosferoo? Ke meta pinoome kati?

(Sto periptero)

Kate Then exi tipota etho. Then vlepo tipota enthiaferon. Pate ke esis stin Anglia?

Nancy Oxi, pame stin Sparti, stin mitera too Ari. Ta pethia mas ine sixna mazi tis stis thiakopes. Avrio pernoome to treno. Kostizi pio ligo.

Kate O anthras sas thoolevi stin Trapeza tis Elathos?

Nancy Ne. I thoolia ine enthiaferoossa ala ta lefta ine liga. Exoome ena thiamerisma, ala ine mikro, ke ena palio aftokinito. Panda xriazete poli thoolia. I ikoyenia moo meni stin Kalifornia ke i fili moo ine stin Floritha ke grafoome pola gramata. THelo na pao stin Ameriki ala ine poli akriva.

••••▶ Page 79

Kate	But you have a beautiful house in Porto Rafti.
Nancy	A house in Porto Rafti? I was never in Porto Rafti. When we have holidays we go to a friend in Pireus.
Tom	Kate, come quickly! We must go. Goodbye! What is the matter, Kate?
Kate	Wait, Tom, wait…!

▶ New words

aerothromio   *airport*
protimo/protimisa   *I prefer/ I preferred*
bori na perimeni   *it can wait*
kanoone   *they do/make*
milane   *they speak*
mitera   *mother*
too   *of*
ke tote?   *and then?*
Xristooyena   *Christmas*
xioni   *snow*
karavi   *boat*
eki kato   *down there*
ti kanete?   *How are you?*
teliosan   *are finished*
iperoxos/i/o   *wonderful*
kseroome   *we know*
too xronoo   *next year*

fandastikos/i/o   *fantastic*
vivlio   *book*
vlepo   *I see*
sixna   *often*
thiamerisma   *apartment*
ikoyenia   *family*
meni   *he/she/it lives or stays*
meno/emina   *I live/I lived*
grafoome   *we write*
grafo/egrapsa   *I write/I wrote*
gramata   *letters*
pote   *never/ever*
otan   *when*
ela!/elate!   *come! (familiar/formal)*
ti simveni?   *what's the matter?*
perimene/perimenete   *wait! (familiar/formal)*

TOTAL NEW WORDS: 33
TOTAL GREEK WORDS LEARNED: 370
EXTRA WORDS: 81

GRAND TOTAL: 451

Kate	Ala exete ena omorfo spiti sto Porto Rafti.
Nancy	Ena spiti sto Porto Rafti? Then imoon pote sto Porto Rafti. Otan exoome thiakopes pame se enan filo ston Pirea.
Tom	Kate, ela grigora! Prepi na pame. Adio! Ti simveni, Kate?
Kate	Perimene, Tom, perimene...!

▶ Learn by heart

This is your last dialogue to learn by heart. Give it your best! You now have six prize-winning party pieces, and a large store of everyday sayings which will be very useful.

Adio!

| Kate | Parakalo. Kalimera kirie Thiamandi. Ime i Kate Walker. Imaste sto aerothromio. Ne, I thiakopes teliosan. I Elatha ine iperoxi. O Tom THeli na sas milisi*. Mia stigmi parakalo, e... adio! |
| Tom | Ya, Pavlo! Ti? Agorases ke ta thio? Ine ena e-mail stin eteria moo? Iperoxa! Efxaristo poli! Too xronoo? I Kate THeli na pai stin Italia ala ego THelo na tho tin THesaloniki. Me tin Edith Palmer? SE PARAKALO! Prepi na pame, lipon, THa sas tho sindoma! Yassas, adio! |

---

*THeli na sas milisi: *wants to talk to you*

▶ Spot the keys

Here is a final practice round. If you have the recording close the book right NOW. This time the key words are not shown. When you have found them see if you can get the gist of it. My answer is on page 90.

This is what you might ask of a taxi driver:

Posa lepta mexri to aerothromio ke poso kostizi?

And this could be the reply:

Eksartate pote pate. Kanonika perni ikosi lepta. Ala an exi poli kinisi ke exi pola aftokinita stin yefira perni toolaxiston triandapende lepta. Borite na thiavasete tin timi sto taximetro. Ine metaksi eksinda ke enthominda evro.

Good news grammar

As promised there is no new grammar in this section, just a summary of all the **Instant** verbs which appear in the six weeks. The second line of each entry is the past tense. The 30 verbs are not for learning, just for a quick check. You know and have used most of them!

	I	you	he/she/it	we	they
	ego	esis	aftos/afti/afto	emis	afti
be	ime	isaste	ine	imaste	ine
	imoon	*isaste*	*itan*	*imaste*	*itan(e)*
buy	agorazo	agorazete	agorazi	agorazoome	agorazoon(e)
	agorasa	*agorasate*	*agorase*	*agorasame*	*agorasan(e)*
can	boro	borite	bori	boroome	boroon(e)
	boresa	*boresate*	*borese*	*boresame*	*boresan(e)*
come	erxome	erxosaste	erxete	erxomaste	erxode
	ilTHa	*ilTHate*	*ilTHe*	*ilTHame*	*ilTHan(e)*
cost			costizi		costizoon(e)
			costise		*costisan*
drink	pino	pinete	pini	pinoome	pinoon(e)
	ipia	*ipiate*	*ipie*	*ipiame*	*ipiane*
do	kano	kanete	kani	kanoome	kanoon(e)
	ekana	*kanate*	*ekane*	*kaname*	*ekanan*
eat	troo	trote	troi	trome	trone
	efaga	*fagate*	*efaye*	*(e)fagame*	*fagane*
fix, repair	ftiaxno	ftiaxnete	ftiaxni	ftiaxnoome	ftiaxnoon(e)
	eftiaksa	*ftiaksate*	*eftiakse*	*ftiaksame*	*ftiaksan(e)*
give	thino	thinete	thini	thinoome	thinoon(e)
	ethosa	*thosate*	*ethose*	*thosame*	*thosane*
go	pao	pate	pai	pame	pane
	piga	*pigate*	*piye*	*pigame*	*pigan(e)*
have	exo	exete	exi	exoome	exoon(e)
	ixa	*ixate*	*ixe*	*ixame*	*ixan(e)*
help	voiTHo	voiTHite	voiTHi	voiTHoome	voiTHoon(e)
	voiTHisa	*voiTHisate*	*voiTHises*	*voiTHisame*	*voiTHisan(e)*
know	ksero	kserete	kseri	kseroome	kseroon(e)
	iksera	*kserate*	*iksere*	*kserame*	*kserane*
like			aresi		aresoon(e)
			arese		*aresane*
live	meno	menete	meni	menoome	menoon(e)
	emina	*minate*	*emine*	*miname*	*minane*
must	prepi				
need	xriazome	xriazosaste	xriazete	xriazomaste	xriazode
	xriastika	*xriastikate*	*xriastike*	*xriastikame*	*xriastikan*

	I	you	he/she/it	we	they
prefer	protimo	protimite	protimi	protimoome	protimoon(e)
	protimisa	*protimisate*	*protimise*	*protimisame*	*protimisane*
say	leo	lete	lei	leme	lene
	ipa	*ipate*	*ipe*	*ipame*	*ipane*
see	vlepo	vlepete	vlepi	vlepoome	vlepoon(e)
	itha	*ithate*	*ithe*	*ithame*	*ithan(e)*
smoke	kapnizo	kapnizete	kapnizi	kapnizoome	kapnizoon(e)
	kapnisa	*kapnisate*	*kapnise*	*kapnisame*	*kapnisan*
speak	milao	milate	milai	milame	milane
	milisa	*milisate*	*milise*	*milisame*	*milisan(e)*
take	perno	pernete	perni	pernoome	pernoon(e)
	pira	*pirate*	*pire*	*pirame*	*pirane*
telephone	tilefono	tilefonite	tilefoni	tilefonoome	tilefinoon(e)
	tilefonisa	*tilefonisate*	*tilefonise*	*tilefonisame*	*tilefonisan*
think, believe	pistevo	pistevete	pistevi	pistevoome	pistevoon(e)
	pistepsa	*pistepsate*	*pistepse*	*pistepsame*	*pistepsan(e)*
wait	perimeno	perimenete	perimeni	perimenoome	perimenoon(e)
	perimena	*perimenate*	*perimene*	*perimename*	*perimenan*
want, would like	THelo	THelete	THeli	THeloome	THeloon(e)
	iTHela	*THelate*	*iTHele*	*THelame*	*THelane*
work	thoolevo	thoolevete	thoolevi	thoolevoome	thoolevoon(e)
	Thoolepsa	*Thoolepsate*	*Thoolepse*	*Thoolepsame*	*Thoolepsan(e)*
write	grafo	grafete	grafi	grafoome	grafoon(e)
	egrapsa	*grapsate*	*egrapse*	*grapsame*	*grapsane*

Say it simply

1 Imagine you are at the dry cleaner's. You want to know if the item you have brought to be cleaned can be done by the end of the day since you are leaving for Athens early tomorrow morning. You also want to explain that the stain may be red wine.

Think of what you could say in simple Greek, using the words you know. Then write it down and compare it with my suggestion on page 90.

2 You are at the airport about to catch your flight home when you realize that you have left some clothes behind in the room of your hotel. You phone the hotel to ask the housekeeper to send the things on to you.

What would you say? Formulate your telephone call and say it. Then write it down and compare it with my suggestion on page 90.

▶ Let's speak Greek

Here's a five-point warm-up. Answer these questions using the words in brackets.

1 Agorasate to thiamerisma? (ne)
2 Kserete ti kanoone ta Xristooyena? (tipota)
3 Pote ithate ton anthra sas? (XTHes)
4 Yati piyenete stin Anglia? (ikoyenia, meni, eki)
5 Pos ine i Elatha? (iperoxi)

In your last exercise you are going to interpret again this time telling your Greek friend what others have said in English. Each time say the whole sentence OUT LOUD, translating the English words in brackets.

6 I fili moo ipe oti... (the holidays are finished)
7 O John ipe oti... (we are going to Venice next year)
8 I yineka moo THeli na kseri... (when you go to Los Angeles)
9 Episis THeli na kseri... (what they said)
10 O anthras moo lei oti... (he cannot come)
11 I Angela then erxete yati... (she works on a boat)
12 O filos moo lei oti... (you are very nice)
13 Episis lei oti... (he wants to have your phone number)
14 Ine kapios poo THeli na kseri... (what you did)
15 I mitera moo lei oti... (she likes the shops)
16 Kanenas then kseri... (where he has been in America)
17 I fili moo then kseroon... (who took the car)
18 Kapios kseri... (how we can go to Thessaloniki)
19 Then ksero... (how much it costs to fix)
20 I Kate Walker kseri... (where you can buy **Instant Greek**)

Answers

1 Ne, to agorasa.
2 Then kanoone tipota.
3 Ton itha xTHes.
4 I ikoyenia moo meni eki.
5 I Elatha ine iperoxi.
6 i thiakopes teliosan.
7 tha pame stin Venetia too xronoo.
8 pote tha pate sto Los Angeles.
9 ti ipan.
10 then bori na elTHi.

11 thoolevi se ena karavi.
12 isaste poli kalos.
13 THeli to noomero too tilefonoo sas.
14 ti kanate.
15 tis aresoon ta magazia.
16 poo piye stin Ameriki.
17 pios pire to aftokinito.
18 pos pame stin THessaloniki.
19 poso kostizi na to ftiaksoone.
20 poo borite na agorasete to **Instant Greek**.

▶ Let's speak more Greek

In your own words

This exercise will teach you to express yourself freely. Use only the words you have learned so far.

Tell me in your own words that...

1 next week it's back to work
2 you don't like to work; you'd rather have more holidays
3 nobody knows that you are in Athens
4 your mother has the number of your mobile phone
5 your vacation in Greece (Elatha) was wonderful
6 you did a lot of sightseeing and ate too much
7 your friend Andonis works for the Bank of Greece
8 he is catching a train to Larisa
9 your wife must go to Athens because her father is ill
10 you would like to go to Rhodes for Christmas, but by boat

Answers

1 Tin epomeni evthomatha prepi na thoolepso/pao piso sti thoolia.
2 Then moo aresi i thoolia. Protimo na exo perisoteres diakopes.
3 Kanis then kseri oti ime stin ATHina.
4 I mitera moo exi to noomero too kinitoo tilefonoo moo.
5 I thiakopes moo/mas stin Elatha itan iperoxes.
6 Itha/ithame pola pragmata ke efaga/fagame para poli.
7 O filos moo/mas o Andonis thoolevi ya tin trapeza tis Elathos.
8 Perni to treno ya tin Larisa.
9 I yineka moo prepi na pai stin ATHina yati o pateras tis ine arostos.
10 THelo/THeloome na pao/pame stin Rotho ta Xristooyena, ala me karavi.

▶ Let's speak Greek – fast and fluently

Translate each section and check if it is correct, then cover up the answers and say the three or four sentences fast!

30 seconds for a silver star, 20 seconds for a gold star.

My company can wait.
Nobody knows where I am.
My mother doesn't have the number of my mobile.

I eteria moo bori na perimeni.
Kanis then kseri poo ime.
I mitera moo then exi to noomero too kinitoo moo.

Next year I would like to go to Kos.
Kos at Christmas for a week? Are there any photos?
No, thank you. I don't see anything of interest.

Too xronoo THelo na pao stin Ko.
Stin Ko ta Xristooyena ya mia evthomada? Exi fotografies?
Oxi, efxaristo. Then vlepo tipota enthiaferon.

Hello, what are you doing here? What's the matter?
I need to repair my car and my flat. They are very old.
Can you help me, please – with 200 euros?

Ya sas. Ti kanete etho? Ti simveni?
Prepi na ftiakso to aftokinito ke to thiamerisma moo. Ine poli palia.
Borite na me voiTHisete, parakalo – me thiakosia evro?

Now say **all** the sentences in Greek without stopping and starting. If you can do it in under one minute you are a fast and fluent winner!

Test your progress

Thirty **Instant** verbs have been crammed into this text! But don't panic – it looks worse than it is. Go for it – you'll do brilliantly!

Translate into Greek:

1 We write many letters because we have a computer.
2 Hello, can I help? Your bag is not here? Where can it be?
3 Who knows his number? I am sorry, I don't know it.
4 How are you? I am happy that you do not smoke.
5 Do you want to see Sparti? It's a big town.
6 I do not like January. There is snow and it is often cold.
7 There is a kiosk down there. Would you like something to eat?
8 Why did they not phone? We waited until yesterday.
9 I took the book. He says it is interesting.
10 I believe that the airport is always open, day and night.
11 It is important to know (we) how much the client bought.
12 Have you seen the English newspaper? I do not like the photo. It is ugly.
13 He says that he has a cold. He thinks that he's coming tomorrow.
14 Is an apartment near the centre expensive in Greece?
15 We both have to work. Five children cost a lot.
16 I am going at Christmas. I have holidays in December and not (no) in July.
17 We know Pavlo very well. Do you like him?
18 Can you give me the dog? He is small but nice. What does he eat?
19 Her mother is here. She does not speak Greek. It is a little difficult for her.
20 Don't you know it? It costs 500 euros to fix (we).
21 I must go to the cash dispenser. I need money.
22 I am sorry but **Instant Greek** is finished (teliose).

answers

How to score

From a total of 100%:
- Subtract 1% for each wrong or missing word.
- Subtract 1% for the wrong form of the verb, like 'ime' when it should be 'imoon or imoona' or 'boro pame' instead of 'boro pao'.

There are no penalties for:
- Wrong endings of words, like 'kalos', when it should be 'kali'.
- Picking the wrong word where there are two of similar meaning.
- Wrong word order.
- Wrong spelling, as long as you can say the word!
- Missing out odd little words which might not be translated in English, like 'na, i, to, tis, ton', etc.

> **100% LESS YOUR PENALTIES WILL GIVE YOU YOUR WEEKLY SCORE**

For each test, correct your mistakes. Then read the corrected answers out loud twice.

Week 1 – Test your progress

1 Kalimera, imaste o Ari ke i Jane.
2 Ime apo tin ATHina, ke esis?
3 Poo thoolevete tora?
4 Imoona stin ATHina ton Oktovrio.
5 I fili moo ine stin Elatha ya ena xrono.
6 Panda pame stin Rotho ton Ioonio.
7 Thoolepsa stin Fiat ton Maio.
8 Ti kanete sto Lonthino?
9 Thoolevo se ena skolio.
10 To megalo spiti sto Porto Rafti ine ya ta pethia.
11 Mia stigmi parakalo, poo ine o Aristotelis?
12 Exi to spiti tilefono? Thistixos oxi.
13 Kostizi mia Ferrari poli? Ne, vevea, kostizi para poli.

14 Pos ine i thoolia stin Elatha, kali?
15 O Aristotelis exi mia fili stin eteria moo.
16 Imaste stin Skiatho tris meres tora.
17 Exoome kales THesis sto aeroplano.
18 Panda exo varetes thiakopes.
19 Exi mia omorfi yineka, ena Lamborghini ke pola lefta.
20 Isaste i kiria Onassis? Exete ena megalo aeroplano.

YOUR SCORE: _____ %

Week 2 – Test your progress

1 Poo ine ena tilefono?
2 Signomi, exoome mono pistotikes kartes.
3 Boroome na pame stis epta avrio?
4 Exete ena arketa megalo trapezi? Imaste pende.
5 Ta mikra thomatia then exoone banio.
6 THeloome na fame zambon ke psomakia.
7 Boroome na pame apo tis eksi mexri tis epta para tetarto.
8 Poo boroome na pioome kati etho konda?
9 Imaste sto bar apo tis enea mexri tis theka ke misi.
10 Endaksi, pernoome to Rover ya mia mera.
11 Poso kostizi to proino? Mono theka evro.
12 Ti THelete? To komputer? Then thoolevi.
13 Pos ine i milopita? Kali ala akrivi.
14 Poo ine i tooaletes, aristera i theksia?
15 Boro na pao sto Holliwood.
16 Ena kafe parakalo… pinoome para poli kafe!
17 Poo ine i kiria Pavlithi? Isos sto bar?
18 Eksi evro ya ena krio tsai? Ine ligo akrivo.
19 Imoona stin Rotho ton Fevrooario. Then ine asxima.
20 Ine triakosia bar etho, ena ine trianda metra theksia.

YOUR SCORE: _____ %

Week 3 – Test your progress

1 Prota THelo na pao stin mixani analipsis.
2 Se afto to magazi ta papootsia kostizoone para poli.
3 Ithate ton anthra moo sto farmakio?
4 Imaste etho mexri tis theka ke tetarto.
5 Ithame to tenis stin Anglia stin tileorasi.
6 Lipame ala then exoome to ithio se kokino, se noomero sarandatesera.
7 Afto to magazi then ine ftino.
8 Pios eftiakse to tilefono moo? Esis?
9 Etho ine to polikatastima. Ala then ine anixto.
10 Simera then agorasame para pola pragmata. Mono psomi ke miso kilo vootiro.

11 Ta efaga ola – avga, mila, patates ke ena komati tiri.
12 Prepi na kanoome ta psonia. Ine afto to kendro?
13 XTHes imoona stin eteria mexri tis enea.
14 I Anglikes efimerithes kostizoon poli stin Elatha.
15 Exi leoforio? Oxi? Then pirazi.
16 Itan enas poli kalos politis.
17 Ti ine afto? Kati ya mena?
18 Agorase tin tsanda etho konda i sto Notos Galleries?
19 Ola itane poli akriva. Etsi then agorasa tipota.
20 Xriazomaste tria kila, pistevo.

YOUR SCORE: _____ %

Week 4 – Test your progress

1 Kapios tilefonise ston kirio Thiamandi?
2 THelo na ksero poo ine to estiatorio.
3 Ine arga ke then ine eki. Ti kanoome apopse?
4 Etho ine to menoo! Kserete ta krasia tis Axaias?
5 I mixani analipsis ine epano, piso apo tin eksotho, thipla stin porta.
6 Tin Tetarti prepi na pame ston yatro. Ine ena simandiko randevoo.
7 Yati leo oti ine vareti? Yati tin ksero kala.
8 Ton ithate? Prepi na pao stin Larisa mazi too.
9 O kirios Thiamandis ine pelatis moo. Ta agorase ola.
10 THelo na agoraso afto to pragma. Pos lene sta Elinika…?
11 Tin epomeni evthomatha? Lipame. Then ine thinaton.
12 Borite na me voiTHisete parakalo. Efxaristo poli!
13 Triakosia evro ya thio meres. Poli enthiaferon.
    Ne, fisika to pernoome.
14 Prepi na agoraso tria pragmata ya toos filoos moo.
15 Exo krioma. Xriazome ena yatro.
16 Boroone na fane mono ton baklava?
17 Ine enas apesios skilos. Ti boroome na kanoome?
18 Kanis then ithe pios efaye tin brizola.
19 Boro na po kati: to kotopoolo then ine asximo, ala to psari ine kalitero.
20 Ti pernete? Ta froota? Ne, vevea, ine apo tin Axaia.

YOUR SCORE: _____ %

Week 5 – Test your progress

1 Apagorevete na pate sto estiatorio xoris papootsia.
2 Moo aresi i Porsche sas. Itan poli ftini?
3 Otan ime se thiakopes milao Elinika poli.
4 Xriazome eksi isitiria. Exete mi-kapnizondes THesis?
5 Pistevo oti exoome provlimata me tin mixani.
6 Then moo aresi to Internet. Ine poli thiskolo.
7 Then katalaveno. Borite na milate pio arga parakalo?

8 Kani zesti ke exi kosmo. Pame stin poli.
9 Mia ora mazi tis moo thini ponokefalo.
10 Sta fanaria ine ena leoforio. Poo pai?
11 I pistotiki karta then ine etho. Prepi na tilefonisoome stin astinomia.
12 As to kanoome etsi: prota agorazoome to Ferrari ya mena ke meta to bloozaki ya sena.
13 Moo aresi afto to aftokinito ala to alo itan kalitero.
14 Exoome mono ena litro venzini ke then exi venzinathiko mexri tin ATHina.
15 Moo aresi o ilios ke moo aresi i vroxi. Moo aresoon ke ta thio.
16 Parakalo, imaste ikosi xiliometra apo tin ATHina. Exi kanena garaz?
17 Signomi. Xriazome voiTHia parakalo. Then ksero tin ATHina. Poo ine o staTHmos?
18 O kendrikos thromos? Then ine poli thiskolo. An pernete ton ipoyio.
19 Poo ine? Ti ekanan? Then moo aresi na perimeno.
20 Erxomaste apo tin platforma thekaepta. Poo ine o Spiros?

YOUR SCORE: _____ %

Week 6 – Test your progress

1 Grafoome pola gramata yati exoome ena komputer.
2 Yasas, boro na voiTHiso? I tsanda sas then ine etho? Poo bori na ine?
3 Pios kseri to noomero too? Lipame, then to ksero.
4 Ti kanete? Ime ikanopioimenos poo then kapnizete alo.
5 THelete na thite tin Sparti? Ine mia megali poli.
6 Then moo aresi o Ianooarios. Exi xioni ke sixna kani krio.
7 Ine ena periptero eki kato. THelete kati na fate?
8 Yati then tilefonisan? Perimename mexri xTHes.
9 Pira to vivlio. Lei oti ine poli enthiaferon.
10 Pistevo oti to aerothromio ine panda anixto, mera ke nixta.
11 Ine simandiko na kseroome poso agorase o pelatis.
12 Ithes tin Angliki efimeritha? Then moo aresi i fotografia. Ine asximi.
13 Lei oti exi krioma. Pistevi oti erxete avrio.
14 Ine ena thiamerisma konda sto kendro akrivo stin Elatha?
15 Ke i thio prepi na thoolepsoome. Pende pethia kostizoon poli.
16 Piyeno ta Xristooyena. Exo tis thiakopes ton Thekemvrio ke oxi ton Ioolio.
17 Kseroome ton Pavlo poli kala. Sas aresi?
18 Borite na moo thosete ton skilo? Ine mikros ala kalos. Ti troi?
19 I mitera tis ine etho. Then milai Elinika. Ine ligo thiskolo ya aftin.
20 Then to kseris? Kostizi pendakosia evro na to ftiaksoome.
21 Prepi na pao stin mixani analipsis. Xriazome lefta.
22 Lipame ala **Instant Greek** teliose.

YOUR SCORE: _____ %

Say it simply (Week 6)

1   Signomi, exo ena megalo provlima. Isos ine kokino krasi. Ala then ime
     veveos. Imaste sto ksenothoxio mexri avrio. Pame stin ATHina stis epta.
     Borite na to kanete simera parakalo?
2   Parakalo. Kalimera, ime i Kate Walker. Tilefono apo to aerothromio.
     Imoona sto thomatio ikosithio ya tris meres. Lipame ala ine pragmata
     sto thomatio ke tora ime sto aerothromio ke pame sto Birmingham. Borite
     na me voiTHisete parakalo? To ksenothoxio kseri poo meno sto
     Birmingham. Efxaristo poli.

Spot the keys (Week 6)

It depends when you are going. Normally it takes 20 minutes. But if there is a
lot of traffic and a queue on the bridge, it takes at least 35 minutes. You can
read the price on the meter. It will be between 60 and 70 euros.

*This is to certify
that*

. . . .

*has successfully completed
a six-week course of*

Instant Greek

with . . . . *results*

Date   *Instructor*

how to use the flash cards

The **Flash cards** have been voted the best part of this course! Learning words and sentences can be tedious, but with flash cards it's quick and good fun.

This is what you do:

When the **Day-by-day guide** tells you to use the cards, cut them out. There are 24 **Flash words** and 10 **Flash sentences** for each week. Each card has a little number on it telling you to which week it belongs, so you won't cut out too many cards at a time or muddle them up later on.

First, try to learn the words and sentences by looking at both sides of the cards. Then, when you have a rough idea, start testing yourself. That's the fun bit. Look at the English, say the Greek, and then check. Make three piles: for the 'correct', 'wrong' and 'don't know' ones. When all the cards are used up, start again with the 'wrong' pile and try to whittle it down until you get all of them right. You can also play it 'backwards' by starting with the Greek face-up.

Keep the cards in a little box or put an elastic band around them. Take them with you on the bus, the train, to the hairdresser's or the dentist's. If you find the paper too flimsy, photocopy the words and sentences onto card before cutting them up. You could also buy some plain card and stick them on or simply copy them out.

The 24 **Flash words** for each week are there to start you off. Convert the rest of the **New words** to **Flash words**, too. It's well worth it!

FLASH CARDS for Instant LEARNING:
DON'T LOSE THEM – USE THEM!

exoome 1	ne 1
parakal**o** 1	**i**maste 1
tr**a**peza ΤΡΑΠΕΖΑ 1	p**a**me 1
p**a**o 1	ap**o** 1
imoona 1	**i**ne 1
pol**i** 1	**o**morfos 1

yes ¹	we have ¹
we are, we were ¹	please ¹
we/let's go ¹	bank ¹
from ¹	I go, I'm going ¹
he/she/it is ¹	I was ¹
beautiful ¹	very, much, a lot ¹

ti **1**	poo **1**
exo **1**	**t**ora **1**
kalisp**e**ra **1**	kal**o**s/kal**i**/ kal**o** **1**
sign**o**mi **1**	**i**me **1**
y**a** **1**	i thooli**a** **1**
xr**o**no **1**	left**a** **1**

where **1**	what **1**
now **1**	I have **1**
good, nice **1**	good evening **1**
I am **1**	excuse me **1**
the work **1**	for **1**
money **1**	year **1**

2 **ligo**	2 **etho**
2 **aristera**	2 **arketa**
2 **ala**	2 **poso kostizi?**
2 **oxi**	2 **proino**
2 **endaksi**	2 **avrio**
2 **kati**	2 **mono**

2	2
here	little
enough	left
how much?	but
breakfast	no
tomorrow	OK
only	something

2 theksi**a**	2 ke
2 **i**sia	2 ts**a**i
2 logariasm**os**	2 akriv**o**
2 th**i**klino	2 micr**os/i/o**
2 **o**xi **a**sximo	2 pistotik**es** k**a**rtes
2 kr**i**os/a/o	2 kond**a**

2	2
and	right
tea	straight on
expensive	bill
small	double room
credit cards	not bad
near	cold

3	3
simera	pr**e**pi
lip**a**me	leofor**io**
taxithrom**io** ΤΑΧΥΔΡΟΜΕΙΟ	**o**lo
met**a**	TH**e**lo
magaz**i**	m**e**xri
p**o**te	arg**o**tera

must `3`	**today** `3`
bus `3`	**I'm sorry** `3`
all `3`	**post office** `3`
I want `3`	**after, afterwards** `3`
until `3`	**shop** `3`
later `3`	**when** `3`

3 etho	**3** komati
3 xTHes	**3** periptero
3 pios	**3** afto
3 kakos/ia/o	**3** tiri
3 psomi	**3** ftino
3 pragmata	**3** krasi

3 piece	3 here
3 kiosk	3 yesterday
3 this	3 who
3 cheese	3 bad
3 cheap	3 bread
3 wine	3 things

4 ka**p**ios	4 yat**i**
4 ks**e**ro	4 randev**oo**
4 simandik**o**	4 efxarist**o** pol**i**
4 thinat**os**	4 enthiaf**e**ron
4 estiat**o**rio	4 ap**e**sio
4 **a**rostos/ **a**rosti	4 yatr**os**

4 why/ because	**4** someone
4 appointment	**4** I know
4 many thanks	**4** important
4 interesting	**4** possible
4 terrible	**4** restaurant
4 doctor	**4** sick

psari — 4	boro — 4
kreas — 4	salata — 4
nero — 4	kanis — 4
fisika — 4	endaksi — 4
kero — 4	apopse — 4
laxanika — 4	kotopoolo — 4

4 I can	4 fish
4 salad	4 meat
4 nobody/ anybody	4 water
4 all right	4 of course
4 tonight	4 time
4 chicken	4 vegetables

5 aftok**i**nito	5 nosokom**i**o ΝΟΣΟΚΟΜΕΙΟ
5 apagor**e**vete	5 gr**i**gora!
5 gramato- kiv**o**tio	5 isit**i**rio
5 ke ta th**i**o	5 kendrik**o**s thr**o**mos
5 m**e**ra, m**e**res	5 mi- kapniz**o**ndes
5 moo ar**e**si	5 then moo ar**e**si

5	5
hospital	car
5 quickly!	**5** it's forbidden
5 ticket	**5** letter-box
5 main road	**5** both (and the two)
5 non-smoking	**5** day, days
5 I don't like	**5** I like

5	5
pio	stasi ΣΤΑΣΗ
staTHmos ΣΤΑΘΜΟΣ	treno
venzinathiko ΒΕΝΖΙΝΑΔΙΚΟ	yemato
poli	eki pera
proto	ponokefalo
astinomia	ipoyio

5 (bus) stop	5 more
5 train	5 (railway) station
5 full	5 petrol station
5 over there	5 city, town
5 headache	5 first
5 underground	5 police

6 aerothr**o**mio ΑΕΡΟΔΡΟΜΙΟ	**6** mit**e**ra
6 Xrist**oo**yena	**6** xi**o**ni
6 kar**a**vi	**6** per**i**ptero
6 ip**e**roxos	**6** ks**e**rume
6 fandastik**o**s	**6** vivl**i**o
6 sixn**a**	**6** thiam**e**risma

6 mother	6 airport
6 snow	6 Christmas
6 kiosk	6 boat
6 we know	6 wonderful
6 book	6 fantastic
6 apartment	6 often

6 ikoy**e**nia	**6** m**e**no/**e**mina
6 gr**a**fo/ **e**grapsa	**6** gr**a**mata
6 pot**e**	**6** perim**e**nete!
6 kar**a**vi	**6** vl**e**po
6 protim**o**	**6** k**a**to
6 el**a**te!	**6** **o**tan

6 I live/I lived	**6** family
6 letters	**6** I write/ I wrote
6 wait!	**6** never/ever
6 I see	**6** boat
6 down there	**6** I prefer
6 when	**6** come!

Kalimera, ime o/i … ¹

Mia stigmi, parakalo ¹

Pame stin Kerkira ¹

I Patra ine poli omorfi ¹

Thoolevo sto Lonthino ¹

ya tin eteria moo ¹

Poo thoolevete? ¹

Imaste se thiakopes tora ¹

Exoome ena spiti ¹

Imaste stin Elatha ¹
ton Avgoosto

Good morning, I am … [1]

A moment, please [1]

We are going to Corfu [1]

Patras is very beautiful [1]

I work in London [1]

for my company [1]

Where do you work? [1]

We are on holiday now [1]

We have a house [1]

We were in Greece
in August [1]

Exete thom**a**tio? [2]

P**oo i**ne to thom**a**tio? [2]

P**o**so kost**i**zi? [2]

Ti **o**ra? [2]

TH**e**loome na p**a**me stin [2]
ATH**i**na

Stis okt**o** ke mis**i** [2]

Ine pol**i** akriv**o** [2]

Ip**a**rxi **e**na bar eth**o**? [2]

K**a**ti na f**a**me [2]

Ton logariasm**o**, parakal**o** [2]

Do you have a room? 2

Where is the room? 2

How much does it cost? 2

At what time? 2

We want (would like) to 2
go to Athens

At half past eight 2

It is too expensive 2

Is there a bar here? 2

Something to eat 2

The bill, please 2

Pist**e**vo **o**ti… **3**

Pr**e**pi na p**a**me **3**

THe**l**o na p**a**o ya ps**o**nia **3**

Pr**e**pi na p**a**o stin tr**a**peza **3**

M**e**xri p**o**te? **3**

Ip**a**rxi **e**na magaz**i**? **3**

Th**e**n pir**a**zi **3**

Ag**o**rasa pol**a** pr**a**gmata **3**

Ine pol**i** kalos **3**

Kond**a** sto taxithrom**i**o **3**

I believe that... **3**

We must go **3**

I want to go shopping **3**

I must go to the bank **3**

Until when? **3**

Is there a shop? **3**

It doesn't matter **3**

I have bought a lot of things **3**

He is very nice **3**

Near the post office **3**

Iparxi kapios? 4

Then ipe 4

Tin epomeni evthomatha 4

Brosta stin porta 4

Piso apo tin eklisia 4

Then exoome ora 4

Pame na fame 4

Pao mazi too 4

VoiTHia, parakalo 4

Pos lene sta Elinika …? 4

Is there someone? 4

He did not say 4

Next week 4

In front of the door 4

Behind the church 4

We don't have time 4

We are going to eat 4

I('ll) go with him 4

Help, please 4

How do you say
in Greek ...? 4

me epistrof**i** [5]

Lipa**me**, then katalav**e**no [5]

Bor**i**te na mil**i**sete
pi**o** arg**a**? [5]

Ti **o**ra **e**xi tr**e**no? [5]

Ime pol**i** ikanopioim**e**nos [5]

Moo ar**e**si to R**o**ver [5]

Moo ar**e**si yat**i** **i**ne
ken**oo**ryio [5]

Moo ar**e**soone ke ta th**i**o [5]

Then moo ar**e**si to kras**i** [5]

Bor**oo**me na
kapn**i**soome eth**o**? [5]

return (ticket) 5

I am sorry,
I don't understand 5

Can you speak more
slowly? 5

At what time is there
a train? 5

I am very satisfied 5

I like the Rover 5

I like it because it is new 5

I like both 5

I don't like the wine 5

Can we smoke here? 5

Kanis then to kseri

Then to ksero

Ti simveni?

Ti ipe?

Ti kanoone?

Ti kanete?

Then vlepo …

Then ine tipota

I ikoyenia moo meni stin Anglia

Pame se ena filo

Nobody knows it 6

I don't know it 6

What is the matter? 6

What did he say? 6

What are they doing? 6

How are you? 6

I don't see … 6

There is nothing 6

My family lives in England 6

We are going to
a friend's 6